PENGUIN BOOKS

WACKY CAKES AND WATER SNAKES

Stacie Hill Barta owned and operated a catering business in Boston for ten years. She now lives north of Palm Beach with her husband and two children.

WACKY CAKES AND WATER SNAKES

Four Seasons of GREAT Family Activities

Stacie Hill Barta

PENGUIN BOOKS

PENGUIN BOOKS

Published by the Penguin Group
Penguin Books USA Inc., 375 Hudson Street,
New York, New York 10014, U.S.A.
Penguin Books Ltd, 27 Wrights Lane,
London W8 5TZ, England
Penguin Books Australia Ltd, Ringwood,
Victoria, Australia
Penguin Books Canada Ltd, 10 Alcorn Avenue,
Toronto, Ontario, Canada M4V 3B2
Penguin Books (N.Z.) Ltd, 182–190 Wairau Road,
Auckland 10, New Zealand

Penguin Books Ltd, Registered Offices:
Harmondsworth, Middlesex, England

First published in Penguin Books 1995

1 3 5 7 9 10 8 6 4 2

Grateful acknowledgment is made for permission to reprint "Firefly" from
Under the Tree by Elizabeth Madox Roberts. Copyright B. W. Huebsch, Inc.,
1922. Copyright renewed Ivor S. Roberts, 1950. Copyright The Viking
Press, Inc., 1930. Copyright renewed Ivor S. Roberts and The Viking Press,
Inc., 1958. By permission of Viking Penguin,
a division of Penguin Books USA Inc.

LIBRARY OF CONGRESS CATALOGING IN PUBLICATION DATA

Barta, Stacie Hill.
Wacky cakes and water snakes: four seasons of great family
activities/Stacie Hill Barta.
p.   cm.
ISBN 0 14 023387 3
1. Handicraft.   2. Cookery.   I. Title.
TT145.B37   1995
790.1'91—dc20   95–11634

Printed in the United States of America
Set in Stempel Schneidler Light
Designed by Judith Abbate

To my family, with love:

Tred, my husband, for his encouragement.

Lauren and Hunter, my children, for their curiosity, eagerness,
and innocence.

Most of all to my beloved mother, who made my childhood
a wonderful adventure filled with love, patience, creativity,
and laughter.

A Heartfelt Thanks

A book of this magnitude involves so many wonderful people that it would be impossible for me to mention each person who gave time, energy, and creativity to make this a reality. To all of you I say thank you—I couldn't have survived the mountains of research papers, lack of sleep, and late-night hours filled with doubt if it weren't for all of you.

I would like to thank the following people individually, however, for the special gifts that they brought to this project:

To Carla Glasser, my agent—I called you out of the blue, and you gave wings to my ideas.

To my associates at Viking Penguin—to Mindy Werner for believing in me; to Susan VanOmmeren for pointing me in the right direction; and to Carolyn Carlson for her genuine enthusiasm and fine-tuning skills. To Paul Buckley for his artistic vision, and Judith Abbate for her inspirational design.

To Binny Jolly for interpreting my words with her whimsical illustrations.

To my brother Jay and sister-in-law Ginny (who is really more like a sister to me) for their constant encouragement, advice, and support.

To the staff, teachers, and students at Rosarian Academy and the Professional Learning Center. I could never walk down the halls without a friendly "How's your book?" A special thanks to all of you who offered recipes, ideas, projects, and encouragements. Miss Bonnie for your Easter Egg Crayons, Mrs. diMichele for the holiday bingo activity, and Mrs. New for allowing the class to test many of the activities and recipes.

To Brooks Little at the Armory Art School for allowing me to conduct multicultural sessions during the Armory Art Camp.

viii A HEARTFELT THANKS

To Roberta S. Clark from the Commission for Jewish Education of the Palm Beaches for her help with the manuscipt..

To Shepherd and Ellen Odgen from the Cook's Garden, Susanna Laskaris from the Brooklyn Botanical Garden, and Mary Applehof for their input with the gardening sections.

To Robin Harrison and Ann Ruethling from the Chinaberry Book Service for their suggestions for the Good Reading section.

To the helpful people at the reference desk of the Jupiter and Summit Boulevard branches of the Palm Beach County Public Library.

To Geralyn Hoey and her mother for the Wacky Cake recipe.

To Bill and Christi at Mailbox Plus, John, my computer whiz, and the countless others I came in contact with in the course of writing this book who so kindly shared their childhood memories, family experiences, recipes, and activities.

Lastly, to my mother, who was always there with a wealth of imagination on everything from building a skating rink to crafting a sandcastle. Thanks for the Christmas Snow recipe and the Clothesline Game.

To my husband, Tred, for turning his head when the dining room table was piled high with papers, drying projects, and boxes of craft supplies. To my precious daughter, Lauren, for your poem to your brother, for trying countless versions of our Ranch Dressing recipe and your daily patience when Mommy was at the computer. To my little rascal, Hunter—just having you playing at my feet some days kept me going. I wrote this book for you, your sister, and all the children.

To my mother-in-law, Judy Barta, for her inspiring poems.

Stacie Barta
March 28, 1995
Jupiter, Florida

WRITE ME!

I would love to hear from you, the reader. Let me know how you enjoyed the book and any ideas you'd like to see included in future books. Write me at 6230 W. Indiantown Rd., Suite 7-330, Jupiter, FL 33458. You may also contact me by fax: 407-744-4797, or use my E-mail address, sbarta@aol.com. I look forward to hearing from you.

Contents

Introduction

My childhood memories are happy ones. I was born on Martha's Vineyard, a small island off the coast of Massachusetts, during the worst storm the Northeast had seen in fifty years. The snow was so severe that the electricity was off on the whole island, save the hospital—where there were two births and a broken leg!

My parents owned one of the oldest sea captain's homes in Edgartown, as well as a weekend camp on Chappaquiddick, a smaller island on the other side of Edgartown Harbor. Before I was of school age we would often spend the whole week out at our camp, which I (much to the delight of all of the adults) would refer to as "Chappa-cricket." My mother and I spent our mornings taking long strolls along the dunes in search of seagull feathers and beach treasures that had washed ashore the previous day. After lunch Dad and I would perform our ritual of checking the lines on our boats— he the lines of our Matthews, the *Sea Chest,* and I the heavy twine that secured my toy boat to the dock. Once we were certain both vessels were riding comfortably in the water, we would return to the camp. Though our house was very remote, somewhat spartan, and lacking most of the basics (electricity for one!), my mother prided herself on being able to entertain, with the simplest of childhood pleasures, me and any other children who might be visiting. We had fancy Indian headbands made of paper and seagull feathers, tea parties with shells for dishes, driftwood mobiles and a Clothesline Game. We made paper dolls and glued on seaweed for hair, set up our paints on the dock and washed our brushes out in quahog shells filled with seawater! They were the most basic of childhood pursuits, but are to this day the ones that I hold dearest to my heart.

Many years later, when my daughter was two, I introduced her to many of my favorite pastimes. I had sold my catering business before her birth, and was anxious to spend her first years with her doing the same kinds of things I had done years before with my mother. One afternoon a friend was over with her child, and we were discussing the lack of books available with quick, creative, and inexpensive things to do with children. I'll never forget the moment she looked at me and said, "Stacie, you do such wonderful things with Lauren. Why don't you write a book!" I was looking for a career change. . . . I could put together all the ideas that I had, arrange them seasonally, and complement them with poems, recipes, and easy family activities. The ideas came so fast that it wasn't long before I had a notebook filled.

During my research I came in contact with grandparents, parents, teachers, and children eager to share their thoughts with me. At the same time I met grandparents, parents, teachers, and adults anxious to learn simple everyday, seasonal activities that they could share with the children in their lives. People were looking for quick ideas because they worked long hours, often at more than one job, and had limited time to spend with their kids. People were looking for creative ideas because they were tired when they got home, or couldn't think of anything interesting to do. It wasn't long before I realized what a need there was for such a book. A book filled with pleasures that have endured the test of time, with quick and easy things to do that are just right for today and that would appeal to all children whether they live in the city or the country. Activities that would teach them about their earth and the people and creatures that share it with them. Activities that they could cherish, and look back on, and perhaps someday share with the children in their lives.

The seasons of youth are the years when the first memories are made. They are the days our children will look back on. I hope this book helps you make them special.

The Signs

Share these seasonal keynotes with the children in your life.

IT'S SNOWING!

Get up close with Snowflakes! Guarantee kids Super Snow Time this season with easy pastimes like Follow the Leader, Monster Tracks, and a home-built Skating Rink. Make Ice Molds, Snow Angels, and some awesome (and colorful!) Snow Creatures. Thaw out indoors with paper Snowflakes, Hot Chocolate, and some classic sweets.

THE LITTLE "WINTER" GARDENER

Keep winter *green* by forcing flowering branches and indoor bulbs. Preserve Berries and Leaves for your holiday decorations.

HANUKKAH

Celebrate the Festival of Lights with a Dreidel Game, a simple handmade Dreidel, and a Holiday Garland. Surprise those you love with Handmade Soaps and a Holiday Coupon Book—a true gift from the heart. Feast on Grandma's Latkes and yummy Carob Brownies.

COME, LITTLE BIRDS!

Make a Holiday Tree and some edible Ornaments for your feathered friends! Find the bird nests in your area on a Winter Nest Walk.

CHRISTMAS

Ring in the "jolly" days with a Living Christmas Tree. Gauge a tree's age with our simple ring-count. Make homemade snow! Handcraft some ornaments this season with Holiday Clay, Popcorn Balls, and a host of simple garlands. Set your little elves to work with Creative Cookie Tins, personalized gift tags, and one-of-a-kind gift wrap. Great Gifts are waiting to be made with Simmering Scents, Napkin Rings, and a Shake-a-Scene kids can make themselves.

FAMILY PETS

Show your appreciation for your dog or cat's unconditional love with our Favorite Biscuits and Catnip Toy. Keep track of critter chores with a Sticker Chart and a personalized Grooming Kit.

# of Winter

KWANZAA

Join in an African-American celebration honoring family and community. Make a Mkeka—a woven placemat in holiday colors—and Cornbread sweetened with honey.

I DON'T FEEL WELL . . .

When kids are abed or feeling blue, brighten their spirits with some indoor fun. Build structures up to the ceiling with our slotted Building Cards. Play a game of homemade Checkers or My Very Own Game, where kids make up the categories. Learn what goes under (and what doesn't!) in Float and Sink. Make a simple flip book. Stuck in bed? Set up a homemade office right at your feet.

HAPPY NEW YEAR

Did you keep your resolutions from last year? Find out with a Resolution Tree. Countdown to the New Year with Party Hats, Glitter Balloons, and The Clock Strikes Twelve! Make a Chinese New Year Banner and shiny red envelopes to start the year off with coins in your pocket.

BE MY VALENTINE

Fragrant Apple Hearts and lovely Valentines for your one and only! Fill a Victorian Keepsake Box with trinkets of love. Send "sweets" to your Sweetie in our Valentine Heart Basket.

STUCK INSIDE

What is there to do! It's too cold to go outside, and children need some ideas to help pass the hours. Make paper Silhouettes. Stretch rubberbands into decorative shapes with a Band Board. Whip up a batch of Play Dough; lather up in a warm bath with Soap Crayons. Winter days can be dark and dreary—light up your day with gilded Light Catchers. Knock off all of your thank-you notes with a "Fan"-tastic Card. Make jewelry from Bread Dough; or try Papier-Mâché.

A "COOKIE-THON"

A Sugar Cookie and Royal Icing recipe that kids will love. Fill your home with the delicious scent of baking cookies and watch your young artists shine with child-friendly decorating tips.

WINTER WONDERS

ONCE WINTER IS UPON US children seem to go into perpetual motion—playing in the snow, sledding, and so forth—often just to stay warm! The earth, however, appears to sleep, as nature takes a rest under her frozen blanket.

- The days are cold and short, as the earth ends its orbit around the sun
- Frost paints the windows and "heaves" the soil
- Tree branches glisten with ice and cast shadows on the snow below
- Toads, squirrels, bears, and other animals hibernate, snug in their dens
- The willow ptarmigan, with its feathers of white, creeps silently across the snow
- Cardinals, sparrows, chickadees, and other birds hunt for the last of the berries and unsuspecting insects
- Rabbits and deer seek out twigs and the bark of trees for food, protected against the cold by their thick, winter fur
- Moose shed their antlers and seek the safety of heavy timber, as protection against strong winds
- The constellations Orion, Auriga, and Gemini sparkle brightly and dominate the mid-winter sky
- December 21 arrives, the winter solstice—marking the shortest day of the year

It's Snowing!

It's snowing! With these two words a child just about sums up the essence of winter. On go the sweaters, the mittens, the hats, the boots—for there are snowflakes to catch, figures to build, snowballs to throw, and hillsides to slide down!

Snowflakes   (ALL AGES)

Many children don't know that all snowflakes are hexagons, meaning they have six sides, and that no two snowflakes are ever alike! Most ice crystals form flat, platelike structures, though some grow into needles or columns—depending on the air temperature and the amount of moisture present. Help kids get a good look at snowflakes! Dress children in black or dark-colored sweaters and have them hold their arms out to catch the falling snow—or line a shallow cardboard box with a piece of black velvet. Either way, the snowflakes will stand out against the background. See how many different patterns you can find!

Super Snow Time!   (AGES 3 AND UP)

Help the kids maximize their fun outdoors in the snow. Here are some easy ideas for the greatest winter ever!

- Line up several soda cans on a board and try to hit them with snowballs. Place a garbage can or box out in the open and see how many snowballs kids can get in it!
- Play "Follow the Leader" through fresh snow—one person cuts a path through the snow (walk in circles, backtrack, go under and over objects, etc.) and remaining trailblazers must follow their footprints *exactly!*

Good Reading

- Elizabeth Falconer and Sarah Coleridge. *January Brings the Snow: A Seasonal Hide and Seek.* N.Y.: Watts, 1989. (Ages 3 to 7)
- Jane Yolen. *Owl Moon.* N.Y.: Philomel Books, 1987. (Ages 4 to 9)

SNOW

O COME to the garden,
  dear brother,
and see,
What mischief was done
  in the night;
The snow has quite covered
  the nice
apple-tree,
And the bushes are
  sprinkled with
white.

—*JANE TAYLOR*

• Make Monster Tracks through the snow! Cut giant "foot-prints" out of heavy corrugated cardboard (holiday boxes are great for this). Have the child place her foot on each footprint and make a mark with a pencil on either side of the child's foot. Poke two holes at pencil marks. Thread a piece of heavy twine through the holes and tie the footprints to the child's feet. Now make tracks!

• Build a Skating Rink on the frozen ground. Pack snow or use "ice blocks" to make a 10-inch-high circular wall. Fill up the center with a fine mist of water for about 40 minutes—until you have 5 to 6 inches of solid ice. Add more spray as needed to keep surface smooth. (Be sure to thaw out the hose in the basement afterwards!)

Ice Molds
(AGES 3 AND UP)

Save all your half-gallon cardboard milk and juice containers to make great ice structures. Open the "spout" end of the container and fill with tap water. Place containers out of doors until frozen solid. To unmold, place the containers in a basin of hot water for a minute or two. Stack ice blocks together (using snow for mortar) to make awesome structures! Make a Snow Village with buildings of different sizes. Create roadways and add sturdy plastic trucks and cars for added enjoyment.

Snow Creatures   (AGES 3 AND UP)

Make an assortment of frozen creatures this winter. Pack empty buckets and pails with snow to use as molds, or roll giant balls of snow to form basic shapes. Try making a Giant Frog or a Dragon. Add on legs, feet, and other features. Search the house for buttons, plastic lids, and scraps of fabric to use for eyes, ears, and tongues. (See "Simple Fun" project on this page, to the right, for instructions on making tints to color snow—turn the Frog green or make a multicolored Dragon!) Add hats, scarves, and sunglasses. Make hair from old mop heads.

Simple Fun

Let kids "color" pictures in the snow. Fill assorted squeeze-bottles with water and tint each one a different shade with a few drops of food coloring or water-based tempera paint. Make self-portraits or have kids sign their autograph on the snow!

THAW-OUT TIME

Kids will be in and out of the house most winter days. Surprise them with these classic (though naughty) indulgences, and a fun paper craft project.

S'Mores

These are not so nutritious, I know, but what's a winter without toasting marshmallows! If you're without a fireplace—bring out a candle. (Only with close adult supervision.) These are the little pleasures that make such fun memories.

> ½ graham cracker
> ½ plain chocolate candy bar
> 1 marshmallow
> ½ graham cracker

Place chocolate on one piece of cracker. Place a marshmallow on a fork and heat until golden brown. Top the cracker with the toasted marshmallow and remaining cracker. The kids will thank you for giving in—just this once! Yields one S'More.

Simple Fun

Make "Angels" in the snow! Have children (dressed warmly) lie down in the snow on their backs with arms at sides and feet together. Have kids lift their arms slowly to the side, and open their legs wide. The impression left in the snow resembles an angel with wings outspread! Take a picture of each child by his or her angel.

Paper Snowflakes

(Ages 4 and Up)

Children can cut white paper to resemble snowflakes. They look wonderful hung on the Christmas tree, at the window, strung into garlands, or turned into a mobile.

Cut a piece of white paper into a circle of any size. (You can use a compass or draw an outline around a plate to get a true circle.) Fold the circle in half. Fold again, once more, and then again. Cut out small pieces of paper from the folded edges, as well as the rounded edge of the paper. Once unfolded, children will be delighted at the lovely snowflakes they have created. For the most interesting effect have kids cut their circles in different sizes.

Vermont Maple Snow

This is an old New England recipe traditionally made with maple syrup. For a different flavoring children may use vanilla or cocoa powder instead. Arm the kids with bowls and large spoons and let them gather the snow.

> ½ cup whole milk
> 1 tablespoon maple syrup, vanilla, or cocoa powder
> 1 tablespoon condensed milk
> Clean snow*

Stir milk, flavoring, and condensed milk together in a medium-size bowl. Add enough snow to make a thick and slushy mixture when beaten with a spoon. Yields about 1 cup.

*Finely crushed ice may be substituted for clean snow. I have found using a food processor does the best job—place a large handful of ice in the bowl and process for about 1 minute or until all the ice is crushed.

Maple Syrup Candy

Kids will need an adult's help with this recipe, as the maple syrup gets very hot.

> 1½ cups maple syrup
> A candy thermometer

Simple Fun

Make a Bear Den! Help kids make a cozy hideaway using blankets or sheets. Place two chairs back to back a few feet from each other and top with a cover. Extra blankets and pillows on the floor make it really comfy! Provide favorite toys and books for added fun.

Clean snow, or finely crushed ice
A large pan

Boil maple syrup in a heavy, medium-size pan, without stirring, until the thermometer reaches the hard crack stage (300–310° F.). Fill a separate pan with snow. Pour the hot syrup over the snow in ribbons. Once cool, the ribbons can be broken into pieces and sucked on like hard candy.

Hot Chocolate

4 cups whole milk
5 ounces semisweet chocolate
Sugar (optional)

Heat milk and chocolate in a heavy, medium-size pan until chocolate has melted and milk is very hot, but not to the boiling stage. Whisk mixture so that chocolate is well blended. Add sugar if a sweeter taste is desired. Pour into individual cups and serve. Makes four one-cup servings.

Good Reading

Anne and Harlow Rockwell. *The First Snowfall.* N.Y.: Macmillan, 1987. (Ages 3 to 5)

The Little "Winter" Gardener

Young gardening enthusiasts can get discouraged during the winter months with the ground frozen solid and not a bloom in sight. Here are two projects to keep their enthusiasm going.

Spring Blossoms in January!

(AGES 3 AND UP, WITH SUPERVISION)

Children can force branches to bloom indoors and make it look like warm weather has arrived. All kids need to "fool Mother Nature" are some branches from an early blooming shrub or tree, a hammer, and a tub or pail of warm water.

Gather branches about 18 to 24 inches long—ones with lots of flower buds and a bit of curve will make a more attractive arrangement than straight sticks with few blossoms. The best varieties for forcing are forsythia, dogwood, honeysuckle, japonica, mock orange, flowering quince, witch hazel, pussy willow, weeping willow, and winter cherry. Have the children lay the branches on a folded towel and carefully pound the ends of the stems with a hammer. (This will split the branches and allow them to "drink" the water quickly.) Put the branches in a container of warm water and place in a cool, well-lit spot. (The cooler the temperature, the more similar it is to actual springlike conditions and the longer the blossoms will last.) Change the water in the container every two to three days and mist the branches often. Branches will blossom in one to two weeks, depending on the variety of shrub you're using.

Simple Fun

Before a heavy snowfall make "Winter Blankets" for the garden. Have kids gather large armfuls of branches and twigs and lay over bedding areas to protect perennial plants.

Holiday Berries and Leaves

(AGES 4 AND UP, WITH SUPERVISION)

Children can preserve plant material to use in holiday decorations, centerpieces, wreaths, and ornaments. Dip berries in liquid floor wax and lay on newspaper till dry. Hawthorn, holly, and bittersweet work well with this method. Leaves can also be dipped in wax and laid to dry, or children can paint the wax on with a small brush. Ivy, holly, laurel, euonymus, and vinca can be done in this manner.

Forcing Bulbs Indoors

(AGES 3 AND UP, WITH HELP)

Paper Whites

I remember helping my mother plant paper-white narcissus in containers when the cold months of winter were upon us. Their lovely fragrance and bright green stems were a constant reminder that spring was, indeed, not far away! We collected all sorts of clear glass containers and filled them with small pebbles. I remember checking on their progress as the roots began to grow and become visible through the glass.

Children can grow an assortment of indoor blooms during the winter. Fill a container to within ½ inch of the top—gravel, polished stones, glass marbles, or aquarium stones are all good choices. Carefully push the bulbs into the stones, pointed end facing up, and fill the container with water up to the base of the bulbs. Place in a cool location until growth begins, and then move to a sunny location.

Amaryllis

Children can grow amaryllis bulbs indoors in time for Christmas! They take from 7 to 10 weeks, so mark the calendar for early November. Plant several in different pots—those kept at colder temperatures will bloom later in the month. Amaryllis bulbs can be kept from year to year.

CHERRY BLOSSOMS FOR CHRISTMAS

German families traditionally gather cherry branches in early December to enjoy their blossoms on Christmas!

KID-SOURCE

Smith & Hawken
Two Arbor Lane, Box 6900
Florence, KY 41022-6900
1-800-776-3336
Bulbs may be purchased
by mail order. Write for
their extensive gardening
catalogues.

Hyacinth

Single hyacinth bulbs can be forced in a glass, though there are special bulb vases that have been beloved since the Victorian era. Bulbs take about 8 weeks to develop.

Hanukkah

Hanukkah, known also as the "Festival of Lights," is an eight-day winter celebration honoring the Jewish people and their fight for religious freedom. Jewish families begin their Hanukkah celebrations by lighting the first candle of the menorah at sundown. The next night two candles are lit, in addition to the shammash, or "servant" candle. With each successive night another candle is lit, until the eighth night, when all nine candles of the menorah are burning brightly.

The Dreidel Game   (AGES 5 AND UP)

There's nothing like a game of Dreidel to cause the family to gather around at Hanukkah! Any number of players can join in—though with large groups it's a good idea to create teams so players (and especially small children) don't get antsy waiting for their turn. The dreidel, which spins like a top, has four sides and is spun for a kitty of pennies, nuts, or small candies. Each of the four sides has a Hebrew letter on it, representing the first letter of each of the words in the following phrase: *"Nes gadol hayah sham"* (A great miracle happened there). According to an ancient story, when the Jewish people retook their temple in Jerusalem there was an oil lamp that continued to burn for eight days—though there was only enough oil for the lamp to burn for one day. Each of the Hebrew letters written on the dreidel directs the player:

- Nun—player takes nothing from the kitty, and it is the next player's turn
- Gimmel—player takes all of the kitty. Each player puts a token into the kitty, and the game continues with the next player

- Hay—player gets half of the kitty
- Shin—player must forfeit one token, which is added to the kitty

Let's Spin!

Players sit in a circle. Each player may use his or her own dreidel or may share one. Individual players are each given the same number of tokens, and must place one token in the kitty. Usually the youngest player starts, and the game progresses in a counter-clockwise manner. The first player spins and moves according to the letter that is facing up when the dreidel falls. At the end of a round each player must place a token in the middle to replenish the kitty. The game ends when a player has won all the tokens.

Variation 1: The game may also be played for points, as letters in the Hebrew alphabet also have a numerical value assigned to them. Nun—50 points; Gimmel—3 points; Hay—5 points; Shin—300 points; and Pay—80 points. The first player to reach 1,000 points wins the game.

Variation 2: Players may spin the dreidel on a game board. (The inside of a box lid works well.) Divide the inside of the lid into 9 squares, and assign each a number. Players spin the dreidel and add to their score whatever number the dreidel lands on. 100 points wins the game.

A Homemade Dreidel   (AGES 5 AND UP)

There are many lovely wooden dreidels available, though it's great fun for kids to make their own.

> *A cardboard egg carton*
> *A ¼-inch-thick, 3-inch-long dowel (or a bamboo skewer with the point removed)*
> *A black marker*
> *Glue*
> *Assorted tokens (pennies, nuts, or individually wrapped candies)*

Carefully cut out one section from the egg carton. (One of the interior sections works better than those on the end.) Trim the top so that the four sides are even. Turn the section upside-down and write one of the letters—N, G, H, S—on each of the four sides.* Sharpen one end of the dowel and poke through the inside of the egg section. Glue the dowel securely in place with a dab of glue on both the inside and the underside. Allow the glue to dry completely before using.

Note: *Children may also use small, square gift boxes to make their dreidels. Simply insert the dowel into the center of the box. Modify the length of the dowel depending on the size of the box.*

*Children in Israel change the letter "s" to "p," which stands for the Hebrew word "poh," which means "here." They use the phrase "a great miracle happened here," instead of "a great miracle happened there."

Grandma's Latkes

It's customary to serve foods cooked in oil during Hanukkah. Latke (LOT-kuh) is Yiddish for pancake, the quintessential Hanukkah food! Most families serve potato latkes with applesauce, jam, or sour cream, although there are numerous variations—with grated zucchini or carrot, a potato-less yeast latke served with cinnamon and sugar, etc. The list goes on, and they are all delicious!

3 large potatoes
1 small onion
2 eggs
2 tablespoons flour (or matzo meal)
¼ teaspoon salt
Freshly ground pepper
A good-quality olive oil

Simple Fun

Kids can make a simple sugar cookie dough (or buy ready-made dough from the grocery store) that can be cut or molded into festive holiday shapes: menorahs, candles, six-pointed stars, and other holiday symbols.

Peel and grate the potatoes and the onion. Beat the eggs in a medium-size bowl, and add the grated potatoes and onion. Add the flour, salt, and pepper and set aside for about 10 minutes, then pour off any excess liquid that has accumulated. Heat the olive oil in a large skillet over medium-high heat. Drop batter by tablespoons into the hot oil, and cook on one side until the edges are golden brown. Flip pancakes and cook until crisp. Drain on paper towels. Serves four.

Holiday Garlands   (Ages 4 and Up, with Help)

Here's a festive garland to hang for Hanukkah. The shapes may also be hung individually or made into a mobile. There are Hanukkah symbols in addition to the menorah, candle, and dreidel: the six-pointed star, known as the Star of David, is an ancient Jewish symbol and is prominent on the flag of Israel; elephants, which were used by the Syrian army under King Antiochus; and the hammer, which symbolizes Judas Maccabeus.

White construction paper
Waxed paper
Tape
Thick blue and silver yarn
Pencil, scissors, and glue (a nozzle-type bottle works best)
Wire ornament hooks
Ribbon (for garland)
Glitter, beads, small buttons, etc. (optional)

Lay construction paper on a flat surface. Draw a holiday shape on the paper—a six-sided star or a menorah are the easiest shapes to start with, though some older children and adults may want to try one of the Hebrew letters in the Dreidel Game. This drawing will serve as the blueprint for your design. Now tape a piece of waxed paper over the design. This acts as tracing paper—you can see your design under it. On the waxed paper outline the shape of the design underneath with a thin stream of glue. Now take the yarn and place it along your glue line. Allow the yarn to dry completely before gently lifting it from the waxed paper. Children can decorate the shapes with glitter or leave them plain. They may be hung individually or strung on a piece of ribbon as a garland.

Good Reading

Fran Manushkin. *Latkes and Applesauce.* N.Y.: Scholastic, 1992. (All ages)

HANUKKAH GIFTS

Long ago children generally received small gifts of pennies, known as "gelt," or candies for Hanukkah. Today the exchanging of gifts is much more common, and many families enjoy making one-of-a-kind items and giving their handiwork as gifts.

Handmade Soaps   (AGES 4 AND UP, WITH HELP)

These scented soaps are easy for children to make and are wonderful holiday gifts. Nestle three or four in a small box and wrap in decorative paper. Plain brown paper looks especially festive when covered with cut-outs or stamps in holiday colors of silver and blue. Silver paper with blue, or blue paper with silver, are two other winning combinations.

> *1 cup Ivory Snow soap flakes*
> *2 teaspoons hot water*
> *Food coloring*
> *Scent: vanilla, lavender, rose, lemon, or a few drops of perfume*
> *Cookie cutters*

Place the soap flakes in a bowl. Mix the water, food coloring, and scent together in a separate bowl, and then combine well with the soap flakes. Knead the mix with your hands until it is the consistency of wet clay. Pinch off pieces and roll into balls. Or roll out between 2 pieces of waxed paper to a ¼- to ½-inch thickness, and cut into decorative shapes using cookie cutters or homemade templates in desired shapes.

Note: *Try blue-tinted soaps cut into six-sided stars, resembling the Star of David. Wrap in silver paper stamped with similar stars.*

A Holiday Coupon Book (AGES 3 AND UP)

Perhaps no gift from a child is as treasured as a homemade gift. Children can make simple "Coupon Booklets" personalized to please individual family members and friends. A gift to a parent may include an offer to wash the car, walk the dog, or bring breakfast in bed. A gift to a sibling may include coupons for making his or her bed, reading a favorite book, helping with a particular chore, or letting the sibling choose the next video, restaurant, or television program the family enjoys together. (This last one should get adult approval before being included!) Younger children can make simple booklets full of coupons promising a hug, kiss, snuggle, or walk together. Part of the fun of such giving is not just in the receiving but in personalizing the coupons to please particular individuals.

Yummy Carob Brownies

Carob, indigenous to ancient Israel, comes from the seed pods of the tamarind tree. Used widely as an alternative to chocolate, carob contains no caffeine and has less fat, making it not only a tasty but a healthy choice as well. A box of brownies wrapped in holiday paper will be sure to bring holiday cheer to any friend!

> ½ cup butter
> 1½ cups light brown sugar
> 2 eggs
> 2 teaspoons vanilla
> 2 cups unbleached white flour
> 8 tablespoons carob powder*
> 2 teaspoons baking powder
> ½ teaspoon salt
> 1 cup chopped walnuts (optional)

Preheat oven to 350° F. Lightly grease a 9- by 13-inch pan and set aside. Melt the butter in a heavy, medium-size saucepan over low

*Carob powder is widely available in health food stores.

heat. Add the sugar and stir until dissolved. Let the mixture cool, then add the eggs one at a time, and the vanilla, stirring until well blended. In a medium-size bowl combine the flour, carob powder, baking powder, and salt. Stir the dry ingredients into the butter mixture, and add the nuts if desired. Pour the batter into the prepared pan and bake in the middle of the oven for 25 to 30 minutes, or until a toothpick inserted in the middle comes out clean. Cool in the pan before cutting into squares. Makes about 2 dozen Brownies.

Come, Little Birds

Good Reading

- Frans Van Anrooy. *The Bird Tree.* N.Y.: Harcourt Brace Jovanovich, 1966. (Ages 5 to 9)
- Fred Burstein. *Anna's Rain.* N.Y.: Orchard Books, 1990. (Ages 3 to 6)

MIDWINTER

*But cheerily the chickadee
Singeth to me on fence
    and tree,
The snow sails round him
    as he sings,
White as the down of
    angel's wings.*

—JOHN TOWNSEND
TROWBRIDGE

When winter is upon us and the landscape is dusted with snow, birds have a hard time finding something to eat. Children can help their feathered friends by making a Holiday Tree. This not only provides birds with an alternative source of food, but is

a festive addition to the winter landscape. Remember, once children start feeding the birds (the best time is right around Christmas) they should continue until the end of winter. The birds will begin to depend on the food, and it's important not to let them down!

A Holiday Tree   (AGES 4 AND UP)

Birds aren't the only creatures to enjoy this winter treat. Deer and other woodland animals are likely to visit your holiday tree as well. Once an appropriate tree has been selected, children can get busy stringing garlands of popcorn, cranberries, peanuts (in the shell), green peas, raisins, cubes of cheese, and apple chunks. Fill individual bowls with the ingredients, and provide a blunt needle (look for plastic needles at craft stores) and a length of heavy thread for each child. Kids can also individually hang any of the items listed above from an ornament hook. Individual ears of corn, orange slices, and chunks of pumpkin work well too. Don't forget to add some brightly colored bows for a festive touch!

Ornaments for the Birds   (AGES 4 AND UP)

Many holiday displays offer inexpensive straw ornaments for the Christmas tree. We've made them just for the birds by dipping ornaments in melted lard or spreading them with peanut butter before rolling them in birdseed. Miniature stars, reindeers, or angels gently swaying against a winter background will delight any bird (or child!) who happens upon them.

Simple Fun

Look for pinecones during family walks. Bring them home and stuff the openings with peanut butter or lard. Let children stick in a few raisins before rolling in birdseed. Hang on your Holiday Tree or from a tall branch, preferably in front of a window so kids can watch the birds feast on their treat!

City Watch

Urban bird lovers can place their treats on their windowsills!

A Winter Nest Walk

(AGES 3 AND UP)

Take a walk through your neighborhood and see how many nests the children can spot, once the trees have lost all their leaves and the nests are clearly visible. (Check page 114 in the Spring section for the "Build a Bird-nest Buddy" activity. It's especially fun for children to spot a nest they have "helped" build!)

Christmas

Christmas, celebrated on December 25, has become a universal symbol of hope and peace, and as Charles Dickens wrote in his *Christmas Carol*, in 1843, "good will towards our fellow man." For Christians, this is the time they remember that Jesus Christ, the Son of God, came to earth in a lowly manger bed. For many people, Christian or not, Christmas is a time of family—of warmth and love, caring and sharing, carrying on with old traditions and creating new ones.

THE CHRISTMAS TREE

It was in Germany that the evergreen tree first became associated with Christmas. Martin Luther was believed to have been walking home one starry evening before Christmas Eve. Awed by the beauty that surrounded him, he took home an uprooted fir tree and proceeded to decorate it with candles. Whether or not this German legend is actually true is not known, but we do know that by the early 1600s the Christmas tree had indeed become the worldwide symbol of this beloved holiday.

How Old Is That Tree?

Every family has its own special recipe for prolonging the life of their tree. Some add warm water with sugar, while others swear by corn syrup. One family I know adds equal parts warm water and carbonated lemon-lime soda. Whatever recipe you choose, it's a good idea to add additional water every day or two. We fill a plastic pitcher with ice cubes and let the children place these in the

City Watch

Christmas in the city can be magical for children! Take kids "window shopping" one night. Feast on the lights, the decorations, and the holiday sights. Celebrate with hot chocolate afterward!

stand—it's fun and prevents water from dripping all over the gifts under the tree.

Most Christmas tree vendors will offer to cut the trunk of your tree before you take it home. Usually they remove about an inch or more from the end so the tree stays fresher longer and can better drink up the water. Most families don't realize this little "end" piece of wood holds the answer to the age of your tree! Wet the piece of wood, which will cause the wood to swell, making the number of rings more clearly defined. Start counting—each ring represents one year. Most Christmas trees are between 8 and 12 years old:

TRIMMING THE TREE

Decorating the tree with children can be one of the highlights of your holiday if you set a few ground rules beforehand. We take out the kitchen timer and give each child a five- to ten-minute turn to hang ornaments. This prevents many squabbles and allows the kids to take breaks to devote to other activities—and keeps them interested longer!

Daddy's Christmas Snow   (AGES 4 AND UP)

My husband loves putting snow on our Christmas tree. It's a standing joke in our home that he will eventually ask the children and me, "Is it time to put on the snow?" The mixture resembles whipped cream, so warn children not to eat it. My mother handed down this recipe to me from her mother, Nana Litchfield.

1 heaping cup Ivory Snow soap flakes
1 cup warm water
1 teaspoon oil of evergreen, or other holiday fragrance

Combine soap flakes, water, and fragrance in the bowl of an electric mixer. Mix on very low speed until well blended. Whip the mixture on high until stiff peaks form and hold their shape. Spread onto the tips of branches with a spoon. Allow to dry for 24 hours before touching.

Simple Fun

Recycle your Christmas tree after the holidays. Check with your local recycling center to see if your city offers a program, like many towns, to turn trees into wood chips or mulch. Children benefit from observing how all things return to the earth to foster new life.

Holiday Clay

(AGES 3 AND UP)

This cornstarch dough is far superior in texture to salt dough. With careful handling and a protective spray, ornaments made from this dough can last for years. Be sure to write the child's name, age, and the date on the back of each ornament before applying any sealer.

> *1 cup cornstarch*
> *2 cups baking soda*
> *1½ cups cold water*

In a large saucepan, mix together the cornstarch and the baking soda with a whisk. Add the water and stir until smooth. Cook over medium heat, stirring constantly, until the mixture resembles slightly dry mashed potatoes. (Mixture should come to a boil and

Simple Fun

Try a Living Christmas Tree this year! Check local nurseries for living evergreens whose roots are bound in burlap. Families may write or call the Society for Living Christmas Trees for more information: 475 Seminole Avenue, Atlanta, GA 30307, 404-614-0410.

Simple Fun

Turn gift tags into wonderful keepsakes! Purchase plain white or colored labels and let children decorate them. Older children can write messages, greetings, or names as well. Or you can recycle last year's Christmas cards by cutting up the pictures and gluing them onto cut-up 3 × 5 cards.

Simple Fun

Younger children can help place stamps on Christmas cards with close supervision. Provide a damp sponge and instruct them to place the stamp in the upper right-hand corner on the front of the envelope. Don't expect more than a few envelopes from each child however!

start to thicken into a lumpy mass that holds its shape.) Turn out into a dish and cover with a damp cloth. Allow to cool.

Once cooled, turn the dough out onto a surface lightly dusted with cornstarch, and knead until the dough is smooth and elastic. Dough may be stored until needed in a resealable plastic bag and refrigerated for a day or two. If dough feels slightly dry, simply allow to reach room temperature and then knead again until smooth and elastic. Makes about 1 dozen medium-size ornaments.

Shaping Clay

Line baking sheets with parchment paper or foil, and preheat the oven to 350° F. Lightly dust work surface with cornstarch, knead the clay, and then roll it out to ½-inch thickness. Cut dough into shapes with cookie cutters. Transfer cut-out shapes to the baking sheets. Smooth any rough edges with a moistened finger or small utensil. Impressions or designs may be scored on the shape with a toothpick or stick, if desired. Hair may be created by pressing a small piece of dough through the holes of a garlic press. Additional shapes may be "glued" on with a dab of water. If shapes are to be hung, make a hole on the top of each with a plastic straw.

Place baking sheets in the preheated oven, then turn off the oven, and allow ornaments to remain in the oven overnight.

Ornaments may be painted with non-toxic acrylic paint, if desired. When done, spray each side with 3 or 4 coats of a quick-drying, clear acrylic spray for protection. Between holidays, store in a rigid container between several layers of tissue paper.

Simple Trimmings   (AGES 5 AND UP)*

Not all decorations need be time consuming or elaborate. Often the simplest garlands made by small hands are the most treasured and can keep youngsters entertained for short periods of time.

Pasta Garlands

Thread mini pretzels or pasta wheels on brightly colored ribbons. Older children may tie on small ornaments or toys.

*With any project involving small objects, great care should be taken to carefully supervise children.

Pinecones

Adults can cut pinecones crosswise into "flowers." Children may decorate them with glitter or small beads and hang them on the Christmas tree, or add them to holiday wreaths and garlands.

Nuts

For an old-time project, let children wrap individual nuts in paper or small gold or silver foil packets. Nuts may also be painted or gilded, and hung individually or strung into clusters to make wreaths.

School Artwork

Small art projects from school or camp can be put to use as ornaments. Let children pick out their favorites. Be sure to put the child's name, date, and grade on the items. (If you make a habit of putting aside smaller items during the year it makes the job much easier. I keep a large manila folder in the kitchen for just this purpose.)

Popcorn

Styrofoam "popcorn" makes a great garland. Children will find it much easier to thread than the traditional popcorn. The pieces can be strung alone or you can alternate with cranberries and wooden or plastic beads. Almost every household has them on hand this time of year and it's a great recycling project for kids! Try alternating with gumdrops too—for a sweet alternative!

Popcorn Balls

Tie these in colorful squares of cellophane and hang on the tree. Popcorn Balls make great "welcome" gifts for any young— or grownup—visitors that drop by your home during the holiday season.

> ½ cup unpopped popcorn kernels
> 6 tablespoons sweet butter, plus additional for handling
> 1 10-ounce bag marshmallows

Simple Fun

If baking Christmas cookies from scratch is out of the question this holiday, purchase storebought sugar cookie dough. Slice, bake, and let children decorate with icing and sprinkles.

Simple Fun

Children can decorate one-of-a-kind Holiday Napkins. Purchase inexpensive plain napkins and paint with holiday symbols. Use acrylic paint, and heat-set by pressing with a warm iron. (This should be done only with adult supervision.)

Simple Fun

Make up red and green batches of play dough for kids to give as presents. Place in a plastic bag tied with pretty ribbon. Attach a small wooden rolling pin and some decorative cookie cutters, in holiday shapes.

¼ *teaspoon salt*
Toppings: mini chocolate chips, jimmies, colored sprinkles, multicolored candy-coated chips (optional)

Pop the popcorn according to the directions on the container. Set aside. Place the 6 tablespoons of butter in a heavy, medium-size saucepan and melt over low heat. Add the marshmallows and stir, until marshmallows have melted and the mixture is smooth. Pour the mixture over the popcorn and stir to coat well. Butter your hands—and those of any helpers—well, and shape the popcorn mixture into individual balls. Roll the balls in decorative toppings, if desired, then wrap in squares of colored cellophane, tie with ribbon, and hang. Makes about 2 dozen 2-inch balls.

CAN I HELP?

Children love to take an active part in Christmas preparations. From making ornaments to trimming the tree, wrapping presents, and making cookies—let children express themselves in celebration of this joyous holiday. Here are some other ways children can join in.

Creative Cookie Tins (AGES 4 AND UP, WITH SUPERVISION)

Let children decorate plain cookie tins with magic markers or acrylic paints. Collages can be made from some of their smaller drawings as well as pictures cut from Christmas cards or magazines and glued to the tin. Top with any clear acrylic sealer (available in hardware stores).

Goodie Bags (AGES 3 AND UP)

Brown paper bags make great gift bags for home-baked and home-made items. Set kids up with small scraps of holiday paper and ribbon (a great use for pieces too small to wrap with!), magic markers, paints, crayons, and glue.

Creative Christmas Cards (AGES 3 AND UP)

Children's artwork can be turned into wonderful Christmas cards. Personalize your family's card this year by using a child's drawing on the cover of your card. (Families with more than one child can make a collage of several works of art or let kids "draw straws" to see who designs the card each year.) Family photographs make great cards too! Let kids think up an original holiday greeting. Older children can show off their penmanship by addressing envelopes.

A Family Holiday Album (AGES 4 AND UP)

Let children help put together a family Christmas album. Include photos of trimming the tree, caroling, the family meal, and Christmas morning. We started one when the children were born, and they now look forward to taking an active part in recording each holiday.

Family Themes (AGES 4 AND UP)

We like to make each year's celebration a little different. As a family, we think of a theme each year. One year we chose Children's Toys as a basis for all our decorations—we found miniature ornaments in the shapes of bicycles, sleds, drums, and dolls, and used them on the tree, our wreath, and in among the evergreen boughs for our table's centerpiece. We've had Musical Instruments as a theme, complete with tiny sugar cookie drums and horns! This past year we went tropical and made dozens of gold "starfish" and shell ornaments to celebrate our first Christmas together in Florida.

Make note in your family Christmas album of the wreath you used, what ornaments were hung on the tree, and what card was sent. Try to keep all the decorations within the theme of your holiday.

GREAT GIFTS

It seems that Christmas gets more and more commercial as the years go by. Opt out this year and let your children entertain themselves for days by working on handmade gifts. The results are

Simple Fun

Wrap gifts in plain paper and then let children add their finishing touches—suggest cutting shapes out of colored construction paper and gluing them on the sides of the packages.

Good Reading

• Kim Solga. *Make Gifts!* North Light Books, Cincinnati: F&W Publications, 1991. (Ages 6 and up)
• Chris Van Allsberg. *The Polar Express.* Boston: Houghton Mifflin, 1985. (Ages 6 and up)

charming and sure to become an annual tradition. Here are some thoughtful, inexpensive, and fun gifts to make for family and friends.

Simmering Scent (AGES 5 AND UP)

This mixture can be divided up and individually packaged in small plastic bags tied with ribbon, include a decorative label written with these instructions: "Combine ingredients with 2½ cups water and simmer on back of stove for a scentsational-smelling holiday home. Replenish water as needed."

> *Dried peel from 3 oranges**
> *4 cinnamon sticks*
> *10 whole cloves*
> *6 star anise*

*Remove skin from oranges with a potato peeler. Air-dry for one week before packaging. Apple parings may also be dried by the same method, and used in place of the oranges. Scent mixtures should be used at once for optimum fragrance.

Napkin Rings (AGES 4 AND UP)

Children can make delightful napkin rings for the holiday table. Cut paper-towel or toilet-paper tubes into 1½-inch-wide circles and follow the instructions for Papier-Mâché on page 57. Once dry, the rings can be painted and decorated:

- Glue small felt or paper leaves on the outside. Top with tiny pinecones, and "berries" of small red wooden beads.
- Paint rings silver or gold. Add small cardboard stars painted blue.
- Glue rickrack around the ring and top with a decorative bow.
- Older children can label rings with individual names—try writing in gold or silver.

A Christmas Snow Scene (AGES 5 AND UP)

Try making one of these shake-a-scenes every year! Children will love collecting them as well as sharing with their special friends.

> *Small glass jar with screw-on lid*
> *Tiny, waterproof holiday toys, ornaments, etc.*
> *Waterproof glue*
> *White glitter*
> *Fabric or felt, ribbon, or rickrack*
> *Scissors*

Wash and dry the jar. Arrange the scene in the bottom of the jar and glue in place. (Or you can arrange the scene on the lid—I've done it both ways.) Allow to dry overnight. Fill the jar with water to within $1/4$ inch of the top. Add the glitter to the jar. Apply one drop of glue to the inside rim of the lid and securely twist into place. Trim fabric or felt into a circle a bit larger than the lid and glue the fabric onto the top and outside edge of the lid. Glue the ribbon to the outside edge of the lid and allow to dry. A quick shake of the jar will make the "snow" fall on the holiday scene.

Let's Wrap It Up! (AGES 6 AND UP)

Children love to make their own wrapping paper at Christmas. Buy large rolls of brown or white paper and roll out long lengths on the floor. (We have taped lengths to the inside of the garage door as well. Whichever method you choose, be sure to put lots of newspaper down first, and dress the kids in old clothes.) Paper may be sponge-painted or spattered with non-toxic water-based paints.

Large pieces of school artwork can be put to good use now. We always wrap presents to grandparents this way. Tie with raffia, yarn, or ribbon.

Family Pets

Simple Fun

Give the family dog a bath, or help a friend bathe her dog! Once the pooch is nice and clean, play ball together!

Next to family and playmates, a child's best friend is often a dog, a cat, or other pet—a hamster or fish, perhaps. Pets offer children unconditional love and a chance to develop responsibility in caring for a living creature.

A Sticker Chart   (AGES 4 AND UP)

Younger children will need help with daily chores when caring for a pet—a monthly chart with stickers is helpful. My husband and I devised a simple one with four columns. At the top of each column is a picture: a bowl of water, a bag of pet food, a leash, and a brush. Each day a child does one of the chores he or she gets to put a dog or cat sticker in the appropriate column. Naturally we adults join in, though even three-year-old Hunter loves to grab Tiger's brush and give him an occasional "free" grooming.

DOGS

Nearly 35 percent of American homes boast a dog! In 1992 the dog population was estimated at over 52 million, with the Labrador retriever the most popular breed, followed by rottweiler, cocker spaniel, German shepherd, and poodle. The Old English mastiff and Saint Bernard are the heaviest dogs, with males often weighing up to 170 to 200 pounds. At the other end of the spectrum is the Yorkshire terrier, who at four ounces has shoulders measuring only 2½ inches high!

Champ's Favorite Biscuits

While I was writing this book our beloved chocolate Labrador, Champ, died. These biscuits were a treat he looked forward to. Often we make up a batch to give to a friend's dog when we go for a visit. These are adorable cut with "dog bone" cookie cutters, though the dough can also be cut into squares or other shapes as well.

    2 cups whole wheat flour
    ¼ cup cornmeal
    ¼ cup parmesan cheese
    ¼ cup wheat germ
    1 teaspoon bone meal*
    2 tablespoons dried parsley
    2 eggs, lightly beaten
    1 tablespoon canola oil
    ¼ cup chicken broth
    ¼ cup milk

*Available at health food stores, or the vitamin section of pharmacies.

City Watch

Good Reading

I LOVE LITTLE PUSSY

I Love little Pussy.
Her coat is so warm,
And if I don't hurt her,
She'll do me no harm.
So I'll not pull her tail,
Or drive her away,
But Pussy and I
Very gently will play.

—JANE TAYLOR

Preheat the oven to 350° F. Combine the dry ingredients in a large bowl. In a separate bowl, add the eggs, oil, broth, and milk and whisk to combine. Add the egg mixture to the dry ingredients and stir to form a firm dough, adding a bit more broth or milk as needed. Turn out onto a floured surface and knead 2 to 3 times. Allow the dough to sit for about 30 minutes. Roll to a ½-inch thickness and cut into desired shapes. Place the biscuits on cookie sheets and bake about 30 minutes, or until golden. Cool the biscuits on sheets till they are crisp. Store in airtight tins or plastic bags. Yields 5 to 6 dozen biscuits.

CATS

Cats inhabit 32 percent of American households, with an estimated feline population of 63 million in 1992. The most popular breed is the Persian, but the most commonly owned is the American shorthair. The largest cat on record is one Edward Bear, who lives in Australia and weighs a record 48 pounds! Tinker Toy, at 7½ inches long, and 2¾ inches tall, is the smallest cat ever! Ma, a cat from Great Britain, wins the prize for longevity—she died in 1957 after living for 34 years!

Cats figure prominently in folklore and were considered a sacred animal in many ancient religions. While it's considered good luck to own a black cat, legend states it's not wise to cross the path of one!

Ashley's Catnip Toy (AGES 5 AND UP, HELP WITH SEWING)

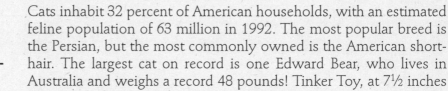

Catnip (*Nepeta cataria*) is an easily grown herb loved by cats. Children who have a cat should make room in their garden for this purple flowering plant. Harvest catnip just as the buds are beginning to open and hang the leaves to dry according to directions in The Little "Fall" Gardener (see page 198). We fold a 4- by 6-inch piece of cloth (tough enough to withstand kitty's sharp claws!) in half and draw a pattern of a fish 3 inches long and 2 inches wide. Stitch along the outline of the shape, being sure to leave enough of an opening at the mouth to stuff the fish full of catnip. With pinking shears, trim the fabric, leaving a ¼-inch border around the stitches.

Stuff the fish with the catnip and close up the opening with a few stitches. You may attach a small bell and a length of ribbon if you desire. Children have great fun pulling the fish along the floor to get their cat's attention.

Grooming Kit   (AGES 3 AND UP)

Kids can put together a simple box full of pet-care supplies. A shoe box or plastic bin makes a good container. Keep a brush, flea comb, and favorite toys inside. Brushes and other items may be labeled with the pet's name by using a waterproof marker or fabric paint. (The fluorescent colors that are known as "puffy paint" or Scribbles work especially well.)

KITTY WISDOM

- When a cat washes its face it is a sign of rain, good weather, or visitors coming!
- An old maritime tale predicts the rise and fall of the earth's waters—if a cat's pupils are closed, it's low tide; if wide open, it's high tide.
- People in Indonesia say if you give a cat a bath it will bring rain!
- Many Africans believe it is bad luck to mistreat a cat.

Kwanzaa

City Watch

Many cities across the country sponsor Kwanzaa festivals during the latter part of December. Check with your local chamber of commerce or the following organization for more information: The African American Dance Ensemble in Durham, North Carolina, 919-560-2729.

From December 26 to January 1, many African-American families celebrate their African heritage with a festival called Kwanzaa (KWAHN-zah), which means "first fruit" in Swahili. Created in 1966 by the African-American scholar Maulana Karenga, Kwanzaa pays tribute to family and community through the seven principles, called Nguzo Saba. Each day a candle is lit in a special candelabra, or kihara (kee-HAH-rah), and one of the principles is observed through discussion and activities.

The Seven Principles

- *Umoja* (oo-MOH-jah)—Unity
- *Kujichagulia* (koo-ji-chah-goo-LEE-ah)—Self-determination
- *Ujima* (oo-JEE-mah)—Collective responsibility
- *Ujamaa* (oo-jah-MAH)—Cooperative economics
- *Nia* (NEE-ah)—Purpose
- *Kuumba* (koo-OOM-bah)—Creativity
- *Imani* (ee-MAH-nee)—Faith

KARAMU

On the last night of Kwanzaa family and friends gather for a lavish feast, known as Karamu (kah-RAH-moo). As Kwanzaa is a cultural rather than religious holiday, African-Americans of different faiths often gather and share stories and songs from their various backgrounds. The dishes served this night further illustrate the rich tapestry of the African-American heritage—with Caribbean, West

Indian, and regional African as well as American foods featured. Many families exchange small gifts, usually handmade or African in origin. Often guests bring favorite dishes to share.

Cornbread

A favorite of young and old, this is delicious served warm from the oven with butter and strawberry jam.

> 1 cup cornmeal
> 1 cup all-purpose flour
> 2 tablespoons honey (or sugar)
> 3 teaspoons baking powder
> ¼ teaspoon salt
> 1 cup buttermilk*
> ⅓ cup unsalted butter, melted
> 1 egg, slightly beaten

Preheat oven to 400° F. and position rack in the middle of the oven. Grease a round, ovenproof dish or pie tin.

In a medium-size bowl, combine the cornmeal, flour, sugar, baking powder, and salt. Set aside. Melt the butter in a small saucepan over low heat. Beat the egg in a medium-size dish. Add the buttermilk and melted butter to the beaten egg and mix, then add the egg mixture to the dry ingredients and stir just until mixed. (There will be a few lumps.) Pour the batter into the prepared pan and bake in the middle of the oven for about 25 to 30 minutes, or until the sides are golden brown and a toothpick comes out clean. Allow to cool in the pan before cutting into 8 wedges.

*If you don't have buttermilk on hand, add 1 tablespoon vinegar to 1 cup of milk.

A Woven Mkeka   (AGES 4 AND UP)

A decorative straw mat, known as a mkeka (muh-KAY-kuh), is used for Kwanzaa, and all the holiday symbols are laid on it. During this harvest festival African-Americans celebrate the fact that "today is a part of yesterday," and the traditional Kwanzaa items reflect this unity. A cup, the *kikombe cha umoja*, is placed on the mat and all sip juice from it to symbolize togetherness. Next the fruits and vegeta-

A SYMBOL OF UNITY

Marcus Garvey created the first African-American flag, or Bendera (behn-DEH-rah) in the early 1900s—red for the struggle for freedom, black symbolizing the unity of the African-American people, and green for the promise of the future.

Simple Fun

Children can make a banner for Kwanzaa using the traditional colors of black, red, and green. Label with this traditional holiday greeting in Swahili: *"Habari gani?"*, meaning "What's the news?"

Good Reading

Deborah M. Newton. *Kwanzaa.* N.Y.: Children's Press, 1990. (All ages)

bles, or *mazao*, are arranged, representing the harvest. Central to this display of the season's bounty is corn, known as *muhindi*. For every child, families place one ear of corn on the mat. The candle-holder, or *kinara*, with the seven candles, *mishumaa saba*, is added next and finally the gifts for the children, known as *zawadi*—for all the promises kept during the year!

A similar woven mat can be made from paper in the traditional black, red, and green colors of Kwanzaa.

3 sheets of construction paper—1 each in black, red, and green
Scissors
Glue or tape

Fold the black piece of paper in half the long way. Starting about one inch in from the end of the paper, cut slits in the paper about ½ inch apart, cutting straight, parallel lines from the folded edge to one inch from the loose ends. Stop making slits about one inch from the other end of the paper. Unfold the piece of paper and lay it flat. You will have a piece of paper with a one-inch border and strips in the middle. These slits are called the "warp." Cut the remaining red and green pieces of paper into lengthwise strips about one inch wide. These strips, which are woven into the warp, are known as the "woof." Using one strip of paper, weave over and under the slits in the black paper. Repeat, using the second-color strip and weaving under and over in the opposite direction of the first strip. Continue weaving with the remaining strips of paper, keeping them close to the edges and to each other. Secure the ends of the strips with a dabs of glue or small pieces of tape. Trim the ends if necessary.

Note: *For a different effect, have children vary the width of space between the warp cuts, or cut the woof strips in random widths. Let kids try cutting in a wavy fashion for a unique look!*

I Don't Feel Well...

Simple Fun

Keep a supply of blank cassette tapes on hand. Set up the tape player anytime a favorite story is read aloud. Tapes are great for children to listen to when sick in bed or during quiet-time.

Children seem to get more ailments in winter than in any other season, perhaps due to the amount of time they're forced to stay indoors due to bad weather. This was certainly the case during the winter of 1993 and 1994. Often adults are at their wits' ends trying to figure out how to keep a sick child in bed or quietly amused.

Building Cards   (AGES 4 AND UP)

Children can amuse themselves for hours with these easy slotted cards. Cut medium- to heavy-weight cardboard into various shapes: squares, rectangles, circles, and triangles. Cut very narrow **V** shape slits about ¼-inch deep in each side of the shape. (This is best done by an adult using scissors or a serrated knife.) Cards may be left plain or painted and decorated with designs. Create various structures by inserting one card into the slit of another. Kids can make buildings, forts, skyscrapers, or imaginary creatures.

Checkers, Anyone?   (AGES 6 AND UP)

The board can be made with colored markers when children are confined to their beds. Kids who are well enough to move around the house may enjoy setting this project up at a table and using acrylic paint.

> *Heavy cardboard*
> *Scissors*
> *Ruler*
> *Waterproof colored markers or paints (red and black are traditional, although any combination will do)*

Small paintbrush
Shellac
¾-inch buttons, 12 each in two different colors (bottle caps, round
  stones, or similar objects may also be used)

Cut the cardboard into an eight-inch square. Mark off the squares into 64 one-inch squares. (There will be eight squares on each side.) Alternately color the squares with two different colors. It's easiest if children go row by row. When beginning a new row make sure the first square is a different color from the square above it. Once the squares are dry (if paint is used) the lines may be redrawn to clearly define the squares. (The board should further be protected with a layer of shellac. Wait until the child has fully recovered, though, or do this away from his or her room, as the fumes are unpleasant.)

Simple Fun

Set up a fancy tray for someone sick in bed. Use colorful napkins and place-mat, flowers, and a small, favorite toy.

Simple Fun

Make a "Tissue Catcher"! This will bring a smile to anyone with the sniffles! Take a large brown paper bag, fold the top over few inches, and staple in place. Draw a face on the front of the bag with its *big* mouth wide open. Cut out the mouth. Decorate the face with construction paper "hair" (wind thin strips around a pencil, unravel, and you'll have "curls" you can glue in place) and draw on features with colorful markers. Great sibling fun!

My Very Own Game
(AGES 7 AND UP)

Children can create their own personal game and tailor questions to a favorite hobby or interest, such as Sports Facts, Favorite Songs or Stories, My School, Science, Holidays, Family Facts, Trivia, and Nature. Half the fun of making this game is having kids think up the questions! The game can be played by two to four players. This game is perfect for the child who is able to get out of bed, but must still stay indoors.

> *40 cards in 4 different colors, 10 cards in each color (let kids pick their favorite colors)*
> *1 die*
> *1 playing board (let children decorate the board to suit the game)*
> *A marker for each player*

Children should decide what topics each color will represent, and write the question and the answer on one side of each card.

Example: Red cards ask questions about animals, birds, and fish.
Question: What fish swims upstream?
Answer: Salmon.

Example: Green cards ask questions about Plants.
Question: What plant eats bugs?
Answer: The Venus Flytrap.

Example: Blue cards ask questions about Food.
Question: What is Popeye's favorite vegetable?
Answer: Spinach.

The last color card is the Penalty card. Drawing that card moves you back two spaces.

Setting Up the Board

Have children draw or paint a winding trail across the face of the game board. Divide the trail into equal 1-inch sections for each move. Color each space one of the four colors of the playing cards.

Let kids decorate the gameboard with cut-out pictures, photos, drawings, or stickers. Mark the beginning of the trail with "START" and the end with "HOME."

Playing the Game

Cards should be sorted according to color. Cards for each color should then be shuffled and placed face down in separate stacks. Children may then roll the die to determine who goes first. The first player rolls the die and moves that many spaces. When a player lands on a color, another person draws the top card of that color and reads the question out loud. If the player answers the question correctly, he may stay where he is. If the question is answered incorrectly, the player must move back to where he was before the roll of the die. Players take turns until everyone has had a turn. The first player to reach "home" is the winner. (For a noncompetitive version players may continue until everyone has reached "home.")

Float and Sink   (AGES 3 AND UP)

Younger children who are able to be "up and about" can learn about the relationship between various objects and water with this simple pastime. It's especially fun to play with two or more children. Gather together a pile of objects such as: a penny, a spoon, a paper clip, a piece of sponge, a cork, a small piece of wood, a small ball, a cotton ball, and so on. Fill a basin or medium-size container with water. Before each item is placed in the water one person asks, "Will it float or sink?" Preschoolers especially enjoy this game, and tell older kids to be ready for some surprises!

"Moving Picture" Books   (AGES 5 AND UP)

Kids can create their own "cartoons" with this easy toy. We buy stacks of small notepads especially for this project at a discount office-supply house.

Have children create an animated story by drawing one scene per page. This works best if kids draw small pictures at the bottom of the page. Try starting in one corner and having the scene "travel" to the other corner with each additional page. Quickly thumb through the pages to see the "moving picture."

Simple Fun

A child can make her own puzzle by drawing a picture on a piece of lightweight cardboard (shirt cardboard is a good choice). Have her cut the picture into pieces and then try to put it back together.

Good Reading

• Anna Pomaska. *Easy Mazes Activity Book.* N.Y.: Dover, 1987. (Ages 4 to 8)
• Laura Joffe Numeroff. *If You Give a Moose a Muffin.* N.Y.: HarperCollins, 1991. (Ages 3 to 7)

KID-SOURCE

Music for Little People
P.O. Box 1460
Redway, CA 95560-1460
1-800-727-2233
This wonderful catalogue
offers a rich selection of
music for children and families, videos, musical instruments, games, gifts, and
toys—many perfect for a
child who is confined to the
house.

A Play Office

(AGES 4 AND UP)

Moms and dads can bring home the following office supplies so kids can set up a play office: old file folders, letterhead, envelopes, Post-it notepads, extra calculators, small boxes, paper clips, stamps, stamp pads, pens, markers, gum stickers. Provide children with a stack of old newspapers or magazines as well. Kids can cut out words to make their own mastheads and memos.

Happy New Year

It's with noisemakers, confetti, and silly hats that we welcome in the New Year—though most children are fast asleep when the revelry takes place. Families can plan a small party early in the evening, perhaps at dinner or with dessert, and allow children to pay tribute to the coming year.

A Resolution Tree (AGES 3 AND UP)

Our family brings out the branches we used during Halloween and Thanksgiving (see page 221) and turns them into a Resolution Tree! Roll a piece of colorful construction paper into a cone, and use tape to secure it. Decorate the cones to look like silly hats—children love gluing on polka dots, feathers, jewels, and ribbons. Kids can then pass out the hats and everyone present can write down their resolution(s) for the New Year before hanging them on the branches. It's fun to save the hats from the previous year and see how close everyone came to keeping their resolutions!

Party Hats (AGES 4 AND UP)

Follow the directions above (or turn to page 152 for Shady Characters and some great ideas for hats) and make an assortment of hats for everyone to wear! Hold a contest for the prettiest, the silliest, and the most colorful hat.

"Glitter Balloon" Favor (AGES 5 AND UP)

Kids can make a colorful party favor to welcome the New Year.

Simple Fun

Cook up Black-eyed Peas and Rice for a prosperous New Year! (Cook rice according to directions on package. Heat one can of black-eyed peas, and add to rice mixture along with one seeded and chopped tomato.) Peas are said to resemble "coins" and ensure a good supply of pocket change in the coming year!

Simple Fun

• Play "The Clock Strikes Twelve!" Set several timers for 10 to 15 minutes and hide them around the house. Let kids search for the timers before they ring.
• Pile 12 blown-up balloons (one for each month) on a couch or chair. See how many kids can pop by sitting on them before the timer goes off! Only "sitting" allowed—fingernail popping is a no-no! Two to three minutes is a good time to allot—depending on age and skill.

Simple Fun

Make homemade confetti! Give kids hole-punchers and a stack of colorful papers, foils, wrapping paper. A great addition to "Glitter Balloon" Favors.

Lightweight acetate
Scotch tape
White glue
Two ½-inch corks
Confetti, glitter
Colorful balloons
Ribbon, feathers

Cut a 2½- by 10-inch rectangle from a sheet of acetate (available at craft and art supply stores), roll into a long tube with a ½-inch diameter, and run a piece of Scotch tape along the seam to seal. Place a dab of glue on the sides of the cork and poke it in one end to seal the tube. Fill the tube with purchased confetti and colored glitter. Seal the other end with the other cork. Blow up a large balloon, knot the end, and tie it to one end of the tube with a colorful ribbon. Tie on additional ribbons and feathers. Place "dots" of white glue on the balloon and sprinkle it with additional confetti and glitter if desired.

CHINESE NEW YEAR

No one seems to celebrate the coming of the New Year as much as the Chinese. Their holiday lasts for fifteen days! On New Year's Eve families watch the Dragon Parade—complete with firecrackers, clowns, and featuring a long, colorful dragon. Often held up by as many as fifty people, the dragon (which signifies Good Luck) is an intricate bamboo frame covered in either paper or silk.

A New Year's Banner   (AGES 5 AND UP)

Chinese families often seal doors and windows with red banners on New Year's Eve. Red, thought to scare off bad spirits, is a prominent color during the holiday. Children can make similar banners out of red paper or felt. Be sure to decorate banners with the traditional New Year's greeting: *"Kung Hay Fat Choi,"* which means "Wishing You to Prosper!"

Red paper or felt
A cardboard tube
Glue
A black waterproof marker
Assorted decorations—buttons, ornaments, flowers, etc. (optional)
Red cord or ribbon
A thumbtack

Lay the paper or felt on a flat surface. Measure the length of tube and cut the paper so the width is the same as the tube's length; the paper can be as long as you want. Holding the tube lengthwise, glue the top of the paper to the tube and fringe the bottom half. Decorate the banner and write sayings expressing hope and good fortune for the coming year. Traditionally these banners were written with couplets—two lines of poetry that rhyme. Blessings should try to incorporate one or more of the following: luck, food, longevity, health, and peace—such as "may your seasons be

Simple Fun

Make your own Fortune Cookies! Remove fortunes from store-bought cookies, and replace with personal fortunes written on small slips of colorful paper.

healthy, peaceful, and full of joy. Kung Hay Fat Choi." Place cording through the inside of the tube and knot. Banner may then be hung with a thumbtack.

Money Envelopes (AGES 5 AND UP)

Children in both China and Vietnam receive shiny red envelopes filled with money on New Year's. Tucked under their pillows, they are the first thing youngsters reach for on New Year's Day! Children can make their own envelopes to give to family members and friends. All kids need are: nine-inch squares of red paper, a ruler, tape, stickers, and a pen. Have children find the center of the square by drawing an **X** on the paper from corner to corner. Fold all four corners of the paper to the center of the **X**. Open up one corner for the flap of the envelope, and secure the remaining three corners by taping in place. The envelope may then be decorated with stickers and wishes for a prosperous New Year.

Be My Valentine

Stolen glances, blushes, giggles, secret admirers, first loves, and fancy Valentines. All of these come to mind on Valentine's Day. No one knows where the custom of exchanging cards originated, though Esther Howland of Worcester, Massachusetts, is credited with making the first commercial Valentine in America.

MAKING VALENTINES

There's something wonderfully charming and old-fashioned about making homemade Valentines with children. Try setting aside a few hours on the weekend, several weeks before Valentine's Day, to make your cards. Gather together paper doilies, lace, ribbon, glitter, glue, and pens. If you've saved old Valentines, greeting cards, and bits of ribbon, now is the time to bring them out! Traditionally cards were made in red, white, and pink, with touches of other colors for detail, though today anything goes. Here are some ideas to get the children started:

Hearts in a Row   (AGES 4 AND UP)

Three or more hearts can be strung together with ribbon. Cut 3-inch hearts out of paper and cut two parallel slits, about ½ inch apart. Lace a length of ribbon through the slits, and knot the ends. Hearts may be glued in place or allowed to slide along the ribbon.

All That I See   (AGES 4 AND UP)

Cut out a small heart-shaped piece of foil and glue on the inside of a card as a "mirror." Let children use the old-time greeting "Re-

Simple Fun

Make a fragrant "Apple Heart" Valentine to hang on a door. Buy dried apple rings (check holiday displays at the grocery store or try your local health-food store) and thread them on medium-weight wire. Shape wire into a "heart," and tie on a red ribbon.

Simple Fun

Make sugar cookie "hearts." Make one recipe of sugar cookies in the shape of hearts. See page 59. Melt 8 ounces of semisweet morsels and one teaspoon butter together. Stir to combine. Dip half of the "heart" cookie into the chocolate. Place on cookie sheet and refrigerate for 15 minutes until set.

flected in this mirror see, all that is beautiful to me" or think up one of their own.

Good Reading

Tasha Tudor. *All for Love.* N.Y.: Putnam, 1984. (All ages)

Valentine Heart Basket (AGES 8 AND UP, WITH HELP)

Children can make a combination card-basket in the shape of a heart by weaving together two half-hearts! It's not really that difficult once the first strip is done—though children should have some basic weaving knowledge before tackling this on their own, or be assisted by an adult. Shiny paper in white and red makes this very festive, though silver or gold works well too.

Cut out two 4- by 12-inch rectangles from medium-weight paper (use different colors), and fold each one in half the short way. At the folded edge of the paper, divide the area into equal sections by placing a pencil mark every ½ inch. (You will have seven marks.)

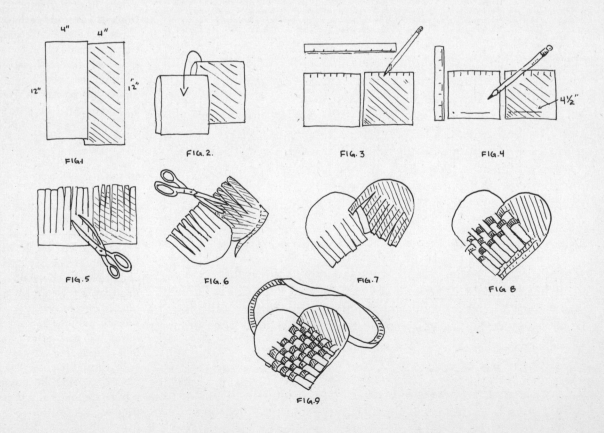

FIG.1 FIG.2 FIG.3 FIG.4

FIG.5 FIG.6 FIG.7 FIG.8

FIG.9

Using these pencil marks as a guide, measure up 4½ inches from the edge and place another mark above each one. Draw lines to connect the marks. (This part is best done by an older child or adult.) Have kids cut along the lines to form eight ½-inch strips. Do the same with the other rectangle. Round off the top of each rectangle. Holding the two halves at right angles to each other, weave the first strip of one half through the first strip of the other half, behind the second one and through the third. Holding securely, weave the second strip under and over (opposite the first strip!) the second strip of the other half. Continue weaving until all the strips have been used. Glue a strip of paper or a piece of ribbon on the inside of the heart to use as a handle. The basket may be filled with small chocolates, nuts, candies, or Valentine favors. Children may opt to decorate their hearts with a holiday greeting or leave them plain.

Note: *These heart baskets may also be made out of felt.*

Simple Fun

Make Victorian Keepsake Boxes for your Valentines! Gather together several small, white boxes and the following decorations: red buttons (use a variety of sizes); lacy white doilies; red, gold, or silver rickrack; costume jewelry or single jewels; and an assortment of Valentine and Victorian pictures (cut-up old cards, magazines—*Victoria* magazine especially—catalogues). Glue the items on the top and sides of the boxes. Add a Valentine, chocolates, spring seed packets, and other tiny keepsakes inside the box as a surprise!

Stuck Inside

There are days during winter, for whatever reasons, that children are confined indoors. Following are some ideas to help pass the hours and keep kids from asking, *"What is there to do?"*

Silhouettes   (AGES 5 AND UP)

Among my favorite possessions is a silhouette done of my mother when she was eighteen years old. Here's a way kids can make similar portraits of family members, friends, and even pets (if they can get them to stay still long enough).

> *2 pieces of 8½- by 11-inch paper, 1 light and 1 dark*
> *Masking tape*
> *A blank wall*
> *A lamp without a shade, or a flashlight*
> *A pencil with a fine point*
> *Sharp scissors with a fine point*
> *Glue or paste*
> *A mat or a frame (optional)*

Tape either the lighter or the darker piece of paper—depending on whether you want your silhouette to be light on dark paper or dark on light—to the wall at eye level. (The piece of paper should be large enough to contain the profile of the subject.) Have the subject sit in a chair close to the paper. Position the light source behind the subject—put the lamp on a table or have someone hold the flashlight. Adjust the light and subject until the profile of the subject is sharp and centered on the paper. Trace the profile on the paper, including as much detail as possible. Cut out the profile (older children or adults) and glue to backing. Frame if desired.

Simple Fun

Make a Draft Lizard! Cut the leg off of an old pair of colorful tights. Fill tightly with clean fabric scraps, old clothing, etc. Tie the end tightly with a piece of yarn or ribbon. Glue on two "button" eyes. Cut out pieces of felt and glue on for nose, mouth, and feet. Make another lizard from the other leg. Place at the base of windows and doors to keep out those chilly drafts.

A Band Board   (AGES 6 AND UP, WITH HELP)

A square piece of wood
Sandpaper
Nails and a hammer
2 to 3 dozen colored rubber bands

Sand the edges of a square piece of wood. With adult help, hammer the nails into the wood in a random fashion or in the shape of a square, circle, triangle, or concentric circles. Kids can make various designs by looping the rubber bands over the nails.

Homemade Play Dough   (AGES 6 AND UP)

This play dough has a wonderful texture. Provide a rolling pin and a variety of cookie cutters for each child. I usually set a timer for 5 to 10 minutes—at the end of that time the children may exchange cookie cutters.

Food coloring
3 cups water
3 cups flour

1½ cups salt
2 to 3 teaspoons cream of tartar
6 tablespoons cooking oil

Color the water with the food coloring to the desired shade and set aside. (Make the shade quite darker than you want it, as it will lighten when combined with the other ingredients.) Combine dry ingredients together in a heavy saucepan and mix well. Add oil and colored water and blend thoroughly. Cook over medium heat, stirring constantly, until a large ball forms. Remove from heat and cool completely. Place on a flat surface and knead until workable. Will keep indefinitely in a resealable plastic bag.

Simple Fun

Make "trees" from old magazines (*TV Guide* or *Reader's Digest* works well). Open to first page, and fold the top right-hand corner down into the seam of the magazine. Crease the fold well. Repeat with remaining pages until all of them have been folded in the same manner. Attach front and back covers together by stapling. "Trees" may be spray-painted green and then dusted with spray "snow." Great as a centerpiece or seasonal room decoration.

Soap Crayons   (AGES 4 AND UP)

After a winter afternoon outdoors in the snow and the cold, there's nothing like a warm bath! These easy soap crayons will keep your budding Renoirs entertained during bathtime, and they clean up easily with water. Make crayons in novelty ice-cube trays with shapes that correspond to the seasons for added enjoyment.

2 tablespoons water
About 1 cup Ivory Snow soap flakes
Food coloring (dark colors work best)
Novelty ice-cube tray

Pour the two tablespoons of water into a 1-cup measuring cup, then fill the cup to the top with soap. Transfer to a medium-size bowl and stir until the mixture resembles a thick, smooth paste. Tint to desired shade with food coloring, stirring well, then place in ice-cube tray, pressing the mixture down with the back of a spoon. Fill each hole to the top. Dry until firm in an airy room. (This usually takes 1 to 2 days.) Remove the soap from the tray and store in a plastic container until needed. Works best on dry surface of tub or tile. Yields about twelve soaps.

Light Catchers   (AGES 6 AND UP)

Winter can be dreary when you're confined to the house and the days are short and dark. Here's a way to make cool pendants, pins, or ornaments that resemble real gold or silver—a sure way to bring a little "sparkle" into the season!

Lightweight cardboard
Cotton string
Silver and gold paint
Acrylic sealer
Buttons, beads
Paintbrushes
Scissors
Glue
Ribbon
Cookie cutters, stencils (optional)

Cut cardboard into desired shapes. (Shapes may be cut freehand or by using a cookie cutter or stencil as a template. Kids can stick to a Winter theme with a deer, evergreen tree, or snow person—or opt for a geometric design.) Raised details may be made by gluing on additional pieces of cardboard or string. (Try coiling, twisting, or braiding short lengths of string for an interesting effect.) Once glue has dried, paint the entire design with gold or silver paint. Apply a coat of sealer to further protect.

For a Pendant: Poke a hole near the top of the design before it is painted. Lace with ribbon or cord. (Put an ornament hook through the hole to make a tree or window ornament.)

For a Pin: Glue fastener (available at craft shops) onto back of design.

THANK-YOU CARDS

Children probably write more notes of thanks during the winter months than at any other time of year. (Save their birth month perhaps.) Here's a fun idea to take the drudgery out of this task and help kids create some "thank-you" cards to remember!

Simple Fun

Make a personal Phonebook or Address Book. Collect photos of favorite people. Glue each photo to a 4- by 7-inch piece of construction paper. Label each page with the person's name, address, and phone number. Punch the left-hand edge of each page with three holes. Make a front and back "cover" for your book. Punch holes in these pages too. Lace together with colorful yarn or ribbon.

THE LETTER

When Sarah's papa was away
from home
a great way,
She attempted to write him
a letter
one day,
First ruling the paper—an
excellent
plan,
In all proper order Miss Sarah
began.

—*ELIZABETH TURNER*

A Picture Says . . . (AGES 3 AND UP)

Have someone take a picture of the child with whatever gift was received—this can be Danielle on her new bicycle, Sam with his new baseball glove, or little Davis with his stuffed bear. (Children too young to write can "make their mark" and leave the rest to adults and older siblings.) Kids can write one or two sentences describing the picture to help them get started.

A "Fan"-tastic Thank You

Cut eight 6- by 2½-inch rectangles out of colorful construction paper. Cut out eight 3-inch circles. (Cut all the rectangles out of one color paper and the circles from another.) Glue a circle to one end of each rectangle. Print one letter (T-H-A-N-K Y-O-U) on each circle. (Kids can also search through magazines or the newspaper for each letter.) Using a hole puncher, punch a hole in the other end of each rectangle. Reinforce holes with circular gummed reinforcements (from office supply stores). Place rectangles in order and lace with a colorful ribbon or piece of yarn. (This card works well for younger children who get tired after writing a sentence or two!)

MODELING MATERIAL

Bread Dough (AGES 5 AND UP)

Children can form wonderful shapes with this no-bake dough. We make pins and pendants for the kids to wear to school. Press the dough through a garlic press for lifelike hair or beards!

> *10 slices white bread, with crusts removed*
> *10 teaspoons Elmer's glue*
> *1 teaspoon liquid dish detergent*
> *Non-toxic water-base paint*
> *Water-base acrylic sealer*

Tear the bread into small pieces and place in a medium-size bowl. Add the glue and the detergent and mix well with your hands.

Simple Fun

Play Secondhand Rose! Have your kids make up "price tags" in the amounts of 1¢, 5¢, and 10¢. Pick a room and let your kids set up a secondhand shop by labeling items with a price tag. (Remove breakable and valuable items first.) Adults then "buy" their selections from the children. Celebrate afterward with a trip to the toy or novelty store and let the kids spend their newfound money!

Knead until dough is no longer sticky. (This will take a while.) Roll the dough between layers of waxed paper to a thickness of ¼ inch. Cut shapes from dough and place on a foil-lined baking sheet. Details may be made by poking or scratching dough with toothpick or similar utensil. Additional pieces of dough may be attached with a dab of glue. Allow designs to dry overnight or longer, depending on the size of the design. Figures may be left plain or painted with a non-toxic water-based paint. When dry, apply a clear coat of sealer.

Note: *Unused dough may be stored in a resealable plastic bag in the refrigerator for up to two weeks.*

Papier-Mâché (AGES 5 AND UP)

Kids can make great figures or holiday piñatas with this child-pleasing craft!

> *Newspaper*
> *Flour and water for homemade paste*
> *A small brush*
> *An inflated balloon or box to use as a base*
> *Crepe paper (optional)*

Rip the newspaper into strips. The easiest way to do this is to fold several sheets of newspaper in half, and rip down from the fold into ½- to 1-inch strips. Mix up the paste. (See below.) Dip the first strip in the paste, being sure to saturate both sides. Lay the strip over the base and continue laying and overlapping strips until the base is completely covered. Gently smooth out any wrinkles with your hands for a uniform surface. Let the first layer dry completely before applying subsequent layers. Be sure to crisscross each layer. If the base layer was horizontal, then top with a vertical layer. After glue has dried, the papier-mâché figure may be painted.

For a homemade paste: Mix together 3 tablespoons flour and 2 cups of water in a small saucepan. Bring mixture to a boil, reduce temperature, and continue to cook until the mixture is the consistency of heavy cream. Add ½ teaspoon of salt to prevent spoilage. Allow to cool before handling.

Good Reading

Margaret A. Hartelius. *Knot Again! The Complete Lanyard Kit.* N.Y.: Grosset & Dunlap, 1993. (Ages 7 and up)

Note: *For a Piñata: Cut a small trap-door in the top before painting the figure. This is easily done with a serrated knife. (Adults only.) Lengths of crepe paper may be cut, fringed, and glued in place to dangle from the piñata, if desired. Overlap strips for the best effect. Fill inside with candies or small novelty items. Hang up and let children whack at piñata with a broom or plastic bat.*

A "Cookie-Thon"

Though adults are wise to encourage healthy snacking and good eating habits in youngsters, what would childhood be if kids couldn't savor the taste of homebaked cookies once in a while! Winter seems the perfect season for a "Cookie-Thon," when children seek out the comfort of a warm house and a quick snack before heading out into the snow again, or curling up with a favorite book or video and some munchies for some "time out."

Try to set aside a few hours after school one day, or during the weekend, and devote it to baking cookies with the children in your life. If you have friends who enjoy baking as well, invite them to join in the fun. The following recipes are some of our favorites.

Sugar Cookies

Children can cut this dough out into favorite cookie-cutter shapes or freeform designs. Leave plain or decorate with Royal Icing. These work well for any celebration when cut into holiday shapes.

1 stick unsalted butter
¾ cup sugar
1 egg
1 teaspoon vanilla
2 cups unbleached white flour
¼ teaspoon salt
½ teaspoon baking powder

Cream butter and sugar till light and fluffy. Add the egg and the vanilla, scraping down the sides of the bowl as necessary. Combine dry ingredients and gradually add to butter mixture. Beat until well

Simple Fun

Send a friend an Edible Message! Bake a Sugar Cookie in a giant rectangle and write a message with icing. Place in a resealable plastic bag decorated with stickers.

Simple Fun

Try "sponge painting" on sugar cookies. Dampen a small sponge (a sea sponge is perfect) and dip in Royal Icing. Try dabbing several colors on top of each other—just be sure to let each color dry first before adding the next layer.

Simple Fun

Make an easy "piping bag" out of a small plastic sandwich bag. Fill the bag half full with icing and close the bag. Snip off one corner of the bag and gently squeeze to release icing.

Simple Fun

Decorate your cookies with Seasonal stencils! Cut a simple stencil out of construction paper. (Make sure stencils are small enough to fit on the cookie.) Place the stencil over each cookie and sift confectioners' sugar over the surface. Try sifting through a lacy paper doily for a snowflake effect!

mixed. Turn dough out onto waxed paper and chill overnight, or for at least an hour, until firm. Roll dough to ¼-inch thickness on floured surface and cut into desired shapes. Transfer to cookie sheets lined with parchment paper or foil. Bake at 325° F. for 8 to 10 minutes, or until pale golden at the edges. Cool on racks before frosting. Makes about 4 dozen.

Royal Icing

16 ounces confectioners' sugar
3 large egg whites

Place ingredients in the bowl of a mixer and beat on high for about 7 minutes. Will keep for up to 1 week in the refrigerator in a covered container. The icing may be tinted with food coloring. Makes 2½ to 3 cups.

The Signs

NATURE WATCH DIARY

Look for these seasonal signs and record them in a Nature Watch Diary. Glue "Spring Blossoms" on a paper tree.

A RAINY DAY PARTY

Raindrop Art, Cloud Pictures—beat the rainy-day blues with these and other fun weather projects. Snuggle in with some Cinnamon Rice Pudding—nothing's more comforting on a drizzly day!

A WINDY DAY

There's nothing like spring breezes to get a child's spirit flying high! We've got Pinwheels that spin, Kite Climbers that soar, and Windchimes that make music as they dance in the air.

HOLI

Transport kids to India for this joyous spring festival! Make paper suns, rainbow Jell-O, and colorful streamers.

Spring has sprung and there's plenty to do.

PURIM

Kids can put on a show with simple holiday noisemakers, paper masks, and fancy crowns. Enter Puppet Mania! Learn how to turn gloves, socks, and cereal boxes into incredible puppets. Make a simple "dancing puppet" starring your fingers as the "legs"! Create a puppet stage.

NORUZ

Sprout seeds the Iranian way to welcome spring!

PASSOVER

Make decorative paper plates, bejeweled cups, and simple paper envelopes in honor of this ancient family celebration. Learn traditional Hebrew words with Passover lotto, and try a yummy Apple-Nut-Cinnamon spread!

EASTER

Hang an Easter Egg Tree with an assortment of decorative eggs—dyed with Blueberries, stenciled, and covered in Patchwork! Make Crayons in egg-shells. Grow a Living Easter Basket! Make tissue paper blooms for an Easter bonnet, and cook up a batch of Easter Nests and Jellybean Eggs to share with friends!

# of Spring

Let's Go a-Mayin'

Make pretty Circle Baskets and May Cones to hold Spring goodies! Build a miniature Maypole and make a crown from living flowers!

Pussy Willow Kittens

Keep an eye out for the pussy willows to bloom! These fuzzy little treasures can inspire some charming art.

The Little "Spring" Gardener

Design a patch of green with Outrageously Humongous vegetables, a Living Tipi, or rainbow-colored radishes! Make fun plant markers, learn how to raise and release Ladybugs and Praying Mantises! Make an Earthworm Ranch. Learn how flowers can do more than look pretty. With flower games and more, junior gardeners will get a jump-start on Spring!

City Kids Go Green

City kids can create an oasis with Highwire Plants and Green Windowsills! Start a community garden, and bring blooms to the sidewalk! Fill your apartment with Silly, Upside Down Plants, Terrariums, and an amazing Crystal Garden!

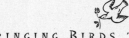

Bringing Birds to Your Yard

Kids can bring birds into their environment with homemade birdseed recipes like Peanut Butter Delight. Make a Bird Cafe, a "Musical" Birdbath, and a Bird-nest Buddy!

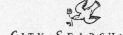

City Search: An Architectural Exploration

Junior draftspeople and architects can take a trip through the world of concrete, brick, and glass in search of Gargoyles, Ionic Columns, and other building elements!

. . . And Baby Makes One More

Big Sister and Big Brother kits. These and other fun "sibling" projects smooth the way for family harmony.

Have a Spring Fling

Celebrate the best of this season with these fun outdoor amusements! Splash through spring puddles on mile-high Tin Can Walkers! Have a race with our charming paper birds in Hop to the Finish. Watch spring happen in ponds and tidepools with our easy Underwater Viewer. Sing and dance with a homemade Kazoo, and wrap up your Spring fling with an Edible Mud Pie as well as real Mud Pies and cookies baked in the sun!

SPRING WONDERS

Children delight in this season of rebirth. A light-hearted time of year, spring represents a fresh start. Much of the world has been asleep under a blanket of snow, but now Spring Fever is in the air, and children all over the world feel the excitement. With the arrival of warm weather, kids can throw off the layers of clothing, rejoice in the natural world, and find happiness in the miraculous events that take place in the spring:

- The days become warmer
- The sun awakens earlier, and stays in the sky longer
- Redwing blackbirds, grackles, tree swallows, sparrows, orioles, warblers, and hawks begin to arrive
- The Blue Azure and Mourning Cloak butterfly drift lazily by
- Leo appears in the southern sky
- Spring peppers and frogs announce their arrival in song
- Snakes slither and warm themselves in the sun
- Buds begin to open—crocus, lilac, forsythia, apple blossoms, dandelions, buttercups, violets, daffodils, snow drops, pussy willows, and pansies say hello
- The maple tree drops its seeds
- Pollen dusts everything and makes us sneeze!
- Pesky mosquitoes buzz around our heads
- The spring equinox delights us: when day and night are equal in length (usually around March 21)

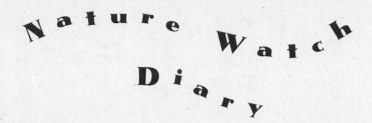

Nature Watch Diary

Children can keep their own personal record of the changes each season with a Nature Watch Diary. By adding notes, drawings, photographs, poems, and small natural treasures, kids can keep in tune with nature.

A spiral-bound notebook with lined pages makes a good diary. Using magazines you have around the house, encourage children to cut out pictures that remind them of the four seasons and guide them in gluing the pictures to the front and back covers. Divide the book into four sections, and label them with the names of the seasons. Help children notice the seasonal changes that occur in their own neighborhood, city block, or park.

Advise kids to write down the date and location of each observance as well, so they can compare happenings from year to year. Reserve a few pages for favorite categories—such as Animals, Plants, Weather, and so on—to make comparisons easier. Children may recognize a pattern year after year—for instance, that robins arrive on a certain date—and can be on the lookout as the date approaches. Keep the diary close at hand so kids are apt to readily use it; when they're kept in a small basket near the door, or on the kitchen counter, kids are more likely to jot down their observations. Try tying an unusual pen or pencil to the book as well for an added incentive. (Younger children can make simple drawings of what they notice, and adults can record their observations for them.)

Good Reading

- Lucille Clifton. *The Boy Who Didn't Believe in Spring.* N.Y.: Dutton, 1973. (Ages 6 to 10)
- Ulf Swedberg. *Nicky the Nature Detective.* N.Y.: Farrar, Straus & Giroux, 1988. (Ages 8 and up)

Simple Fun

Draw the outline of a tree trunk and branches on a piece of brown paper. Cut it out and glue it onto a green piece of paper. Cut an assortment of colored paper into small pieces and let children glue the "spring blossoms" onto the tree!

A Rainy Day Party

Spring showers may bring the flowers, but they have a tendency to dampen young spirits! A party full of drizzly weather fun will put a smile back on little faces.

Raindrop Art   (2 YEARS TO ADULT)

As much as kids complain when showers interrupt their outdoor fun, rainy days can be a cause for celebration. Let's have a Rainy Day Party! We'll start our party off by doing Raindrop Art. Have the kids paint a piece of paper with watercolors, using as many colors as desired. Put aside and go on to something else until the picture is completely dry. Take the dry picture outside during a light rainfall and let the raindrops splash on their artwork. See how the rain has changed the picture? Let the picture dry again. If it is still raining, hold the picture and run through the raindrops again! Pour off excess water and lay flat until dry.

Thunder and Lightning   (5 YEARS AND UP)

Spring has its share of severe weather storms. Chances are you and the kids will hear some thunder this season, and see some bolts of lightning as well. My kids are afraid of the sounds and flashes in a bad storm, so I try to distract them with this simple science project:

- Count the number of seconds between the flash of lightning and the crash of thunder. Divide the number of seconds by 5 for the number of miles away, and by 3 for the number of kilometers away.

Explain that thunder is the sound made when hot air suddenly meets cold air. Because lightning heats the air around it, when that warm air collides with the cooler air—you hear thunder! Point out that you see the lightning first, because light travels faster than sound. (The speed of light is 186,282 miles or 299,792 kilometers per second. The speed of sound is 1,100 miles, or 335 meters per second.) Armed with the comforting knowledge that the lightning and thunder are actually farther away than they think, kids are more likely to settle down to try some of our projects or hear a favorite story!

Simple Fun

Hold a Rain Dance as Native Americans do. Create a fanciful ceremonial headdress, mask, and costume for each child. Invite friends and neighbors to join in the fun.

Look Up at the Clouds!

(ALL AGES, ESPECIALLY 3 TO 7 YEAR OLDS)

My children and I play this simple game on the way to school in the morning when we're stuck in rush-hour traffic, though it's a perfect quiet-time activity any time of day. Instruct children to look up at the clouds around them and see what faces or figures they can find—a dinosaur or a rabbit wearing boots! Have them try to locate each other's "cloud pictures" as well. Explain that this must be done quickly—as the clouds move, the pictures will change too.

My Cloud Picture

(AGES 3 AND UP)

Small children love to create their very own fuzzy white clouds in a blue sky.

> *Blue construction paper*
> *White polyfill or cotton balls*
> *Elmer's glue*

Instruct children to glue "clouds" onto their blue sky. Little ones love to hang these pictures in their room.

Cinnamon Rice Pudding

Our version of this old-fashioned "nursery food" is a simple stovetop method. Warm and comforting, it's a childhood classic and perfect treat for a rainy day.

3 cups milk
3 tablespoons sugar
Pinch of salt
1 teaspoon vanilla
6 tablespoons uncooked rice (do not use instant rice)
$1/4$ teaspoon cinnamon (optional)
$1/4$ cup raisins (optional)
Nutmeg (optional)

Place the milk in a heavy, medium-size pot. Add the sugar, salt, and vanilla. Stir to blend and bring to a boil. Lower the heat, and stir in the rice. Cover the pot and cook for about 1 hour and 15 minutes, stirring occasionally, until the milk is almost absorbed. The mixture should bubble gently—adjust the heat accordingly. Remove from the heat and stir in the cinnamon and raisins. Cover the pot and allow the pudding to set at room temperature for about 10 minutes. Serve warm in individual pudding cups with a sprinkling of nutmeg, if desired. Pudding may also be refrigerated and served chilled.

A Windy Day

Spring is known for her frisky gusts of air and is the perfect time of year for some wind-related projects. So let the breezes blow and get ready for some outdoor fun!

Pinwheels   (AGES 5 AND UP)

Children can make simple pinwheels out of paper and mount them on the eraser end of a pencil. Computer paper works well, though any medium-weight paper will do. Kids can color the paper first with markers if they desire. Show younger children how to blow at the pinwheel to send it spinning—you'll get the best results by blowing from the side instead of the front, or take the pinwheel outside and let the wind do the job.

> *Paper*
> *Ruler*
> *Pencil*
> *Scissors*
> *Straight pin*
> *Two ¼-inch wooden or plastic beads*
> *An unsharpened pencil with a fat eraser on the end*

Cut a 6-inch square out of the paper. Find the center of the square by drawing two diagonal pencil lines through the square from corner to corner. Where the lines intersect is the center of the square. Cut along the pencil lines to within 1¼ inch of the center. Bend each corner in to the center (these four corners are marked A in the illustration), being careful not to fold the paper—corners should curve into the center of the square. Thread a bead onto the straight

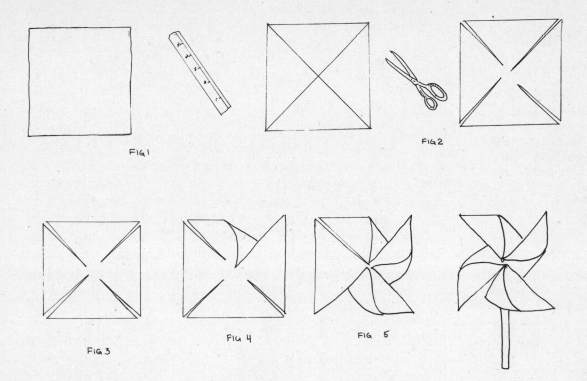

FIG 1 FIG 2 FIG 3 FIG 4 FIG 5

pin and stick the pin through the first corner. Continue adding corners to the pin until all four are threaded on. Poke the pin through the center of the X. Thread the remaining bead onto the pin and push the pin into the eraser. Fat, decorative erasers from novelty stores work best—the eraser should be thick enough so none of the pin protrudes. Adjust the pin so that the pinwheel spins freely. Hold the pinwheel aloft on a windy day and watch it spin!

Kite Climber (AGES 6 AND UP)

For directions on making a kite that will really fly, contact your local library, where there are many wonderful books that have detailed kite-making instructions. Here's an easy toy that kids can make—a Kite Line Climber. This spinning contraption, also called a "message" or a "kite fairy," can be made in a matter of minutes and will work its way—magically!—up the kite string.

City Watch

Meet some friends in the park and have a kite-flying contest! Award simple prizes for the highest and the lowest flyer, the funniest looking, and the most colorful.

Kids can add one or more of these to their kite string and watch them climb up to the sky! Try making different colored climbers.

Posterboard
Plastic straw
Pencil
Scissors
Tape

Cut a 6-inch circle (using a compass or tracing the outline of a small plate) out of the posterboard. Poke a hole in the center of the circle. Cut three slots in the circle: one 3-inch slot from the outside edge to the center hole, and two 2-inch slots from the edge. Bend up a wing next to each slot. Cut the straw in half. Slit the length of the straw with the scissors and push the straw through the middle of the circle. Tape the straw in place on both sides of the circle, being

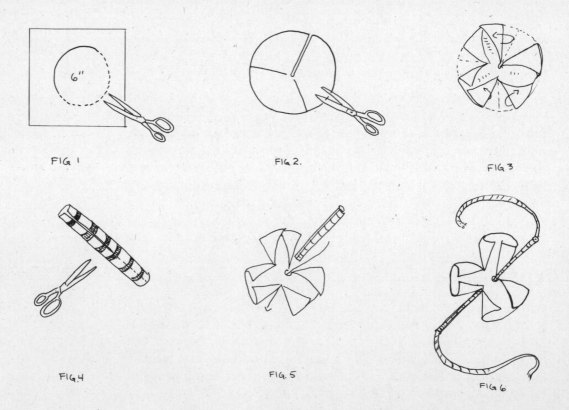

FIG 1

FIG 2.

FIG 3

FIG.4

FIG. 5

FIG 6

sure to line up the cut in the straw with the 3-inch cut in the circle. Slide your kite string through the lengthwise slit in the straw and watch it climb for the sky!

Windchimes

(ALL AGES)

Children can "make music" with the wind when they build a simple windchime. Have kids experiment with different items—each will give a different sound. Make sure that the items hang near each other so that the slightest breeze will cause them to touch. Some types of windchimes to consider: A Kitchen Clatter—try hanging spoons, cookie cutters, measuring spoons (individual) and cups. Nature's Way—tie shells, stones, or beach glass onto strings. Try hanging hollow 4- to 6-inch lengths of bamboo for a deeper sound.

Found items
A coat hanger
Yarn or dental floss

Lay out your found items. Tie a 12-inch length of yarn to each item. Hook the coat hanger on a doorknob or some other sturdy holder and begin to tie the items onto the cross piece of the hanger. This is an as-you-go-along process—the windchime not only has to be balanced, but the items will have to be arranged until a pleasing sound is achieved. Take away or add items on each end until the windchime is balanced. Once kids like the arrangements of items, make sure all of the knots are tight. Hang the windchime where it is most likely to catch the breeze. Suggest making several different chimes—then sit back and enjoy the music!

BEAUFORT WIND SCALE

1 to 3 mph—smoke will slowly drift
4 to 7 mph—leaves rustle gently (perfect kite-flying breeze)
8 to 12 mph—leaves toss, small flags flutter
13 to 18 mph—trees toss, dust and paper fly
19 to 24 mph—trees bend (kite string will break)
25 to 31 mph—too strong to play outdoors!

Simple Fun

Toddlers can blow like the wind and use their breath to create some great works of art! Pour 1 teaspoon of brightly colored paint on a piece of paper. Let kids blow (hard!) through a drinking straw to create designs on the paper.

H o l i

Simple Fun

Make a Rainbow! Attach a nozzle to a hose and turn it to the fine mist setting. With your back to the sun hold the hose overhead. A rainbow will appear like magic!

Holi, also known as the Fire Festival, is the most important Spring festival throughout India. Celebrated during the Hindu month of Phalguna (March), the festivities last anywhere from three to ten days.

Indian children love to hear the legend surrounding this happy celebration: There once was an Indian god named Hanuman who was very, very hungry. He was so overcome with starvation that he ate the sun. At once the world became dark. People were sad and unhappy without any sunshine to cheer them. One of the other gods thought of a wonderful solution. He combined colored powders and water and gave the pretty mixture to the people to throw at each other. Soon the air was filled with laughter and the people were happy once again. As the people celebrated and threw the powders on each other Hanuman watched. He couldn't help but laugh at their antics and suddenly opened his mouth. Out came the sun and the world had light once again. Spring had truly arrived!

Indian children throw a rainbow of colors on each other during Holi, either in powdered form or as a liquid in bamboo blowers. There is dancing and singing to the music of the horns and drums. Huge bonfires are lit by the light of the moon, as all over India the night is filled with an orange glow. Once the fires have burned out, Indian children and adults mark their foreheads with ashes to ensure good luck in the coming year.

Let's Celebrate Holi!   (ALL AGES)

- Children can cut a Sun out of yellow construction paper and decorate it with colorful markers and crayons. Glue strands of tissue paper and ribbon around the edge for "rays." Attach a string and hang on the window.

• Make up 2 or 3 batches of brightly colored Jell-O. When partially set, layer in a clear dish and top with whipped cream and colored sprinkles!

• Send the kids outside and let them throw small bags of colorful confetti at each other.

• Tie or glue long streamers onto heavy cardboard wands. Try yellow (the symbol of spring), as well as traditional Holi colors like red, orange, and green. Encourage children to run so that the wind catches their streamers.

Purim

Purim, or the Feast of Lots, is one of the Jewish holidays most loved by children. Held in early spring, on the fourteenth day of Adar (March), it is a celebration of thanksgiving and rejoicing in Queen Esther's victory for the Jewish people over the evil prime minister, Haman. People make offerings to the poor and gifts to the children. In the synagogue the holiday takes a merry turn, as Jewish children are allowed to dress in masks and costumes and to rattle noisemakers (graggers) whenever Haman's name is mentioned. The Megillah (Scroll of Esther) is read, and the story often told as a play or puppet show. Children especially love to eat Haman-taschen—pastries that are traditionally filled with either poppy seeds, apricot preserves, or chopped prunes and raisins. Triangular in shape, they symbolize the three-cornered hat worn by Haman.

Graggers   (AGES 3 TO 8, WITH HELP)

Children can make simple noisemakers with two small paper plates. Staple them together all around the edges, leaving a small opening. Fill the inside with dried pasta, beans, or small stones, then staple the opening closed. Provide the children with colorful markers, crayons, bits of paper or cloth, stickers, sequins, and glue for decoration. Some children like to glue streamers on—try curling ribbon or crepe paper around a pencil for curly streamers.

Try tin can shakers too. Use a can with a plastic lid—peanut and yogurt-covered raisin containers are perfect for this. Cover the outside of the can with felt, fabric, or paper. Cut out pictures from paper or felt that resemble some Purim symbols—beautiful Queen Esther; Mordecai, the good minister and Esther's cousin; or evil Haman and his black, triangular hat. Fill the inside of the can as above and replace the plastic lid. Instruct kids to shake their graggers whenever Haman's name is mentioned!

A Purim Show   (ALL AGES, YOUNGSTERS WITH HELP)

Children enjoy acting out the story of Purim and the triumph of good over evil. Encourage the children to put on a play in home-made costumes or stage a puppet show. Celebrate afterward by having a parade or visiting loved ones.

Masks

Make simple masks from paper plates. Cut holes for the eyes and decorate with features and hair resembling a Purim character. Glue handles to the bottoms so children can hold the masks up in front of their faces.

Crowns

Fancy crowns can be cut out of cardboard and covered with foil. Glue on bright paper "jewels" for decoration. Measure each child's head and staple the ends of the crown together to fit.

Finger Puppets

Old gloves can be turned into easy finger puppets. Cut the fingers from the gloves and glue on decorative pieces of fabric, felt, or yarn for clothing and hair. Draw features on the fingertips with markers.

Hand Puppets

Larger hand puppets can be made out of old socks. Glue or sew on two large buttons for eyes. Draw on features, and attach yarn for hair. Clothing and accessories can be made from fabric or felt. Glue on a pink or red tongue and make the puppet "talk" by moving your fingers.

Simple Fun

3- by 5-inch cards make great "dancing" puppets. (These are my daughter's favorite!) Draw a simple outline of a person or animal. Color in the features, hair, and clothes with crayons or markers. Cut out the outline of the figure, leaving extra space on the bottom. Then cut two finger holes in the bottom third of the paper, and fold backwards. Have kids put two fingers through the back of the puppet for legs. Kids may glue on tiny shoes or tie ribbons on fingertips for decoration.

FIG. 1

FIG. 2

FIG. 3

Little raisin boxes can come alive too. Cut out the bottom from an individual serving–size box. Paint or cover the outside of the box with paper. Glue or draw on facial features and hair. Glue a wooden popsicle stick inside the box for a handle.

Small cereal boxes make wonderful "talking" puppets. Carefully open top of box and remove cereal. Cut box in half crosswise by slitting across the front and two sides. Bend box back in half. Paint or cover the exterior of the box with paper. Decorate as for other puppets. Place fingers inside box to make the puppet talk.

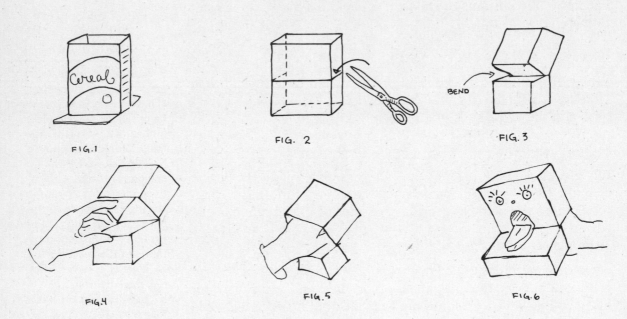

FIG.1 FIG. 2 BEND FIG. 3

FIG.4 FIG.5 FIG.6

Puppet Stage

A simple puppet stage can be made from a large appliance-size cardboard box. Cut out a large square opening from the front for the stage. Poke a hole in each of the upper corners of the opening to attach the curtain. Measure the length of the opening and add 3 inches, then cut two panels of fabric for the curtains. Cut a length of string 2½ times the width of the opening. Make a sleeve for the string in the top of each panel by folding over about 1½ inches of fabric and gluing or sewing in place. Thread string through sleeve.

(The easiest way to thread the curtain is to tie one end of the string onto a safety pin and then push through to the other end.) Thread string through the holes and tie the curtains on the inside of the box, and adjust the length as needed. Children can leave the box plain or decorate it with paints and glitter.

Good Reading

Miriam Chaikin. *Make Noise, Make Merry: The Story and Meaning of Purim.* N.Y.: Clarion Books, 1983. (Ages 5 and up)

Noruz

The first day of spring in Iran, March 21, also marks the first day of the new year. Noruz, which means "new day" is celebrated for twelve days. (This tradition goes back more than 2,500 years!) Families prepare for the holiday months in advance—starting with a good "spring cleaning." Iranian families celebrate by buying new clothes and serving a special Noruz meal composed of seven foods that begin with the letter *s*, symbolizing the virtues of Allah. One of these foods is Sabzeh, the sprouted seeds that are the symbol of spring.

Sprouting Seeds   (ALL AGES)

Iranian children plant their seeds two weeks before Noruz. Help your children sprout some seeds to welcome spring. Cress (*Lepidium sativum*) is perhaps the easiest crop for a child to grow, though barley, celery, lentil, or wheatgrass seeds will work too. (See Kid-Source on page 105 for mail-order details.) All children need is a handful of seeds, water, paper towels, and a shallow container of some sort. A pie tin or large saucer is fine, though using a plastic truck or a doll's bed will be more fun.

Moisten a few paper towels and lay them flat in the container. Have kids sprinkle the seeds on top. In a day or two the seeds will split and the tiny sprouts will begin to emerge. Keep the seeds moist by spritzing them with a plant mister or by adding a few spoonsful of water. Once the seeds have sprouted, kids can add them to a sandwich—or throw them to the wind, as Iranian children do, to symbolize the departure of bad fortune and the happy prospect of the New Year.

Variation

Children can grow seeds in different shapes too! Have them draw a shape on the top of a large, flat sponge. (Cookie cutters come in handy for this or let them draw freehand.) Cut the shape out with scissors or a serrated knife (adults only), moisten it, and lay it in a shallow container. Sprinkle seeds over the sponge and proceed as above. Soon the seeds will sprout to form the shape!

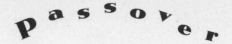

Passover

Passover is a holiday rich with symbols. There are many activities children can do that are not only great fun, but that will help them learn the true meaning of this ancient springtime festival.

A Seder Plate (AGES 3 AND UP)

Central to the Passover meal (the most important Jewish family meal of the year) is the Seder plate laden with the five symbolic foods: a roasted lamb bone, parsley, horseradish or bitter lettuce, a hard-boiled egg, and Haroset—a delicious mixture of chopped apples, walnuts, cinnamon, and honey.

Younger children can make a similiar Seder plate using a paper plate, markers, bits of colored paper, and glue. Show the children how to divide the plate into five sections and let them create their interpretation of the five Passover foods.

Passover Lotto (AGES 6 AND UP)

Older children can play a matching game with the foods and the Hebrew words. Print the following five words on individual 3- by 5-inch cards: *Zeroah, Karpas, Moror, Beitzah,* and *Haroset.* (There is more than one way to spell these words. Use the spelling that your family is most familiar with.) Take five additional cards and let the children either draw or cut out pictures representing the five foods. Help the kids match the words to the proper foods.

Afikomen Cover (AGES 3 AND UP)

Matzoh, an unleavened bread, is always served at Passover. A small piece (the afikomen) is traditionally broken off and hidden inside the house. Children delight in making simple covers for the afikomen. The easiest method is to fold a colorful piece of paper into an envelope and let the children decorate it with markers, bits of felt, or pictures they have cut out. (See page 48 for instructions on making an envelope.) Older children might enjoy making a cover as a simple sewing project. Check your local library for beginner books on sewing.

Haroset

Children love this yummy mixture. Try it on top of warm bagels for a tasty snack.

> *2 apples, cored, peeled, and finely chopped*
> *¼ cup minced walnuts*
> *1 teaspoon cinnamon*
> *2 teaspoons mild honey*

Combine ingredients. Also good as a topping for pancakes or waffles.

Simple Fun

Children can make a Kiddish Cup from a plastic wineglass for the Seder meal. Stemmed glasses are the most attractive and make the children feel especially grown-up on this evening. Provide pretty stickers as well as colored jewels, small stones, and scraps of rickrack for decoration.

Easter

Easter is the most important Christian holiday. It follows Good Friday, when Christians remember Christ's death on the cross.

On Easter morning, Christians believe, Christ rose from the dead. Like Christmas, though, Easter has many secular traditions associated with it. Mention Easter, and children's eyes light up at the thought of scampering through the bushes in search of brightly colored Easter eggs and diving into gaily decorated baskets filled with jellybeans, marzipan, chocolate bunnies, chicks, and lambs!

Easter Egg Tree   (ALL AGES)

This holiday tree makes a wonderful centerpiece for a family dinner. Every spring my children and I make one or two new ornaments to hang. Pussy willow, forsythia, or cherry branches work well for the base of the tree—if you know anyone who has these growing, ask permission to snip a few branches, or order several branches from a local florist. Once cut, bring the branches indoors and mash the ends of the branches gently. Place them in a tall vase or container filled with warm water. Let the children, toddlers too, decorate the branches with hollow egg ornaments, tiny baskets (kids can fill baskets with straw or excelsior and top with a few colorful jellybeans), pastel bows, and small toy animals.

Egg Basics

As these eggs are used as ornaments year after year, they must be hollow. The simplest method is to bring the eggs to room temperature first. With the blade tip of a small, sharp pair of scissors (or

Simple Fun

Cut egg shapes out of pastel-colored paper. Let kids decorate them with gummed stars, dots, and reinforcements from an office supply store. Glue finished eggs onto cards and send to friends at Easter.

with a big needle), make small holes at both ends of the egg. Make sure the inner membrane is broken. Hold the egg over a dish, and blow the contents out. (Save the eggs to make an omelet!) Rinse the inside of the egg with running water, and allow to drain on several layers of paper. Once the eggs are dry, they may be decorated using any of the following methods. After decorating, the eggs may be hung by tying one end of a length of dental floss to half of a toothpick pushed into the top hole of the egg. This "anchor" will take hold and provides an easy method for hanging.

Cracked Eggs
(AGES 3 AND UP)

Younger children work best with hard-boiled eggs, though a few want to try their hand at hollow eggs. Most likely, a few eggs will break in the process. These cracked eggs can be salvaged and turned into adorable containers for tiny Easter animals. Simply trim

Simple Fun

Make pretty Mosaic eggs! Thin white glue with water till it is the consistency of milk. Rip colored tissue paper into ½-inch pieces and let the kids attach the pieces to the eggs with a paintbrush and the thinned glue.

the edges with a pair of nail scissors, and let the children glue tiny rabbits, chicks, lambs, or jellybeans inside. Suggest adding tiny bits of grass, straw, or dried flowers as well. Place in the crook of branches, or glue a piece of ribbon to opposite edges for hanging.

Easter Crayons   (Older Kids, with Supervision)

Speaking of eggshells, here's another fun project that puts all of those broken bits of crayons to good use. We've used eggshell halves for the containers since it's Easter, though the wax may also be poured into mini muffin tins as well. These rainbow-colored crayons are especially loved by toddlers and younger children (who find the chunky shape easy to use) and are a super addition to an Easter basket.

> Assorted crayon stubs, in various colors
> Coffee can, or other clean tin can
> Eggshell halves, rinsed and patted dry

Let kids peel the paper away from the crayon stubs. Place crayon pieces in the can and melt, without stirring, in a double-boiler over simmering water. (There will be little bits of crayon that don't melt, but this is all right.) Place the eggshell halves in an egg carton, and then fill them to the top with the melted crayon wax. Let crayons sit undisturbed until they are hard. (You may place the crayons in the freezer to speed up the process.) Let children crack away the shell to expose their Easter crayons.

Note: *Wax may also be poured into mini muffin tins. Line tins with paper cupcake holders first. Once they are cool, children may peel away paper.*

Blueberry Eggs   (Ages 5 and Up, with Supervision)

My children get a kick out of using fruits, vegetables, and flowers to color some of their eggs. My son loves blue, and fondly refers to this method as Blueberry Eggs! (This method may be used for hollow eggs as well as hard-boiled, though these eggs are not considered edible due to the long cooking time.)

Eggs
2 cups dye
1 tablespoon vinegar
Water

Place the amount of eggs kids wish to dye in a pot. (No more than six.) Add the dye material (see below for suggestions), vinegar, and water to cover. Bring to a gentle simmer, and process for 15 minutes. Remove from the heat and allow to steep in the dye bath for 1 hour. (We do four batches at a time, each with a different dye material. Kids get impatient, and this way they can get down to decorating the first batch, which is the part they like the best!) Once the eggs have cooled, carefully pat dry, and decorate, or rub gently with cooking oil (or bacon, as the Germans do!) to give the eggs a beautiful luster.

Natural Dye Materials

Blue—Blueberries; the outer leaves of red cabbage
Brown—Coffee grinds; tea
Green—Spinach; carrot tops; tansy
Pink—Fresh shredded beets; juice from frozen raspberries
Purple—Marjoram blossoms; red and pink sorrel blossoms
Red—Red onion skins
Yellow—Dandelion or marigold petals; goldenrod; onion peels; turmeric (1 tablespoon per cup of water)

Stenciled Eggs   (AGES 5 AND UP)

Kids love making stencils for decorating their eggs. Have kids cut small shapes out of paper, or have them use any natural objects at hand such as miniature leaves, herb sprigs (parsley and coriander work well), or tiny spring flowers such as violets. Gently place the stencil on the egg. (Moisten the object with a dab of water. It "glues" the stencil in place.) Cut off the toe from an old pair of pantyhose and carefully place the egg inside, making sure the stencil is in place. Tie the top securely with a piece of string, and place in the dye bath. Once the egg is cool, remove it from the stocking and gently peel off the stencil. The stencil shape will be white while the rest of the shell is colored.

Wax Designs   (AGES 3 AND UP)

Have kids draw designs on the egg with a white wax crayon. (This works best on hard-boiled eggs.) Dye the egg as usual. The crayon will work as a wax resist. Children especially love writing their name or a secret message, and then seeing it appear! (See page 228 for invisible ink.)

Good Reading

Patricia Polacco. *Rechenka's Egg.* N.Y.: Philomel Books, 1988. (Ages 3 to 8)

Patchwork Eggs   (AGES 3 AND UP)

Kids can achieve a patchwork design by wrapping eggs with rubberbands or thin lengths of masking tape. Dye as above. When the egg is dry, remove the rubber bands, revealing a pattern of white lines.

Easter Nests and Jellybean Eggs

These sweet little nests will enchant children at Easter and are a favorite holiday treat of my children. Kids love to help shred the cereal, shape the nests, and carefully place the eggs. A wonderfully easy recipe, and a fun addition to a child's Easter basket.

> 8 large Shredded Wheat biscuits
> ¹/₂ cup (1 stick) unsalted butter, plus additional for handling
> 35 large marshmallows
> ¹/₄ teapoon yellow food coloring
> 1 teaspoon vanilla
> Assorted colored jellybeans

Line 2 cookie sheets with waxed paper and set aside. Carefully shred the Shredded Wheat biscuits into a medium-size bowl. In a large pan, melt the butter over low heat. Add the marshmallows, turn the heat to medium, and whisk the mixture until completely melted. Remove the pan from the heat and add the food coloring and the vanilla. Whisk again to blend. Add the Shredded Wheat and stir with a large spoon. The mixture will be stiff—keep turning until the cereal is well coated. Butter your fingers and, working quickly, spoon out about a tablespoon of the mixture. Form into a round "nest," making a small indentation in the middle with your finger. Keep buttering your fingers as necessary to keep mixture from sticking to your hands. Allow nests to dry completely. Fill with assorted colored jellybeans. May be made up to two weeks in advance. Store in airtight containers between layers of waxed paper. Makes about 36 nests.

Note: *Nests may be served on a flat tray, or may be individually boxed or wrapped in tissue for baskets.*

A "Living" Easter Basket   (AGES 3 AND UP)

Kids love the novelty of having a living Easter basket to hold all their goodies! Start this project about ten to twelve days before Easter so that the grass will have a chance to grow.

Line the bottom of a straw basket with a piece of tinfoil. Have the liner come up the sides at least 2 inches all around. Top the foil with a handful of small stones and about 1¹/₂ inches of soilless potting mix. Sprinkle ryegrass seeds (available at garden centers or by mail order) over the mixture and moisten well with a plant mister. Place the basket in a warm, sunny spot. Have children mist the seeds daily. In about 1 week kids will have grass growing inside their Easter baskets.

Fancy Flowers   (AGES 6 AND UP)

No Easter celebration would be complete without lovely straw bonnets. Children can make tissue paper flowers to decorate the crown.

Tissue paper in assorted colors
Ruler
Pencil
Scissors
Straight pin
Decorative beads
Thin craft wire

Stack several layers of tissue paper together and cut into 4-inch squares. Place about 5 squares together, one on top of the other (blossoms may be all one color, though different colors together look especially festive), and fold into a 2-inch square, folding twice. Scallop or fringe the outer edges of the square with scissors and unfold the blossom. Cut a 4-inch length of wire. Poke two holes in the center of the blossom with the straight pin, being sure to go through all the layers of tissue paper. Bend the wire into a "bobby-pin" shape and thread on a few beads. Run the ends of the wire through the holes in the middle of the blossom and twist to secure. Pinch the tissue paper at the base and fluff the layers into petals. Attach the blossoms to a straw hat by running the wire through to the inside and twisting ends.

Let's Go a-Mayin'

May Day isn't celebrated today as much as it should be. What other holiday permits children to ring someone's doorbell, and then go run and hide? Long before the Middle Ages children collected flowers and fashioned them into simple nosegays to be hung on the doorknobs of friends and neighbors. Once they had knocked on the door, they would run and hide in the bushes. Children today can celebrate the coming of Spring by making festive baskets and cones, filling them with flowers and treats and going a-Mayin'.

Have on hand bits of ribbon, lace, fancy stickers, sequins, glitter, glue, pens, and markers to decorate with. Old greeting cards and pretty pictures in magazines are nice to glue on as well. Filled with tiny goodies, the baskets are lovely to share with family, friends, neighbors, and teachers. Seasonal treats to consider: small "spring" animals—bunnies, lambs, chicks, mice; gaily wrapped candies; fairies; pretty stickers; small tubes of glitter; tiny bundles of sequins (tie up in a small square of leftover fabric and secure with a ribbon); and miniature bouquets of flowers. (To keep the flowers fresh, wrap the ends of the stems in a wet paper towel. Cover the towel with a piece of aluminum foil. You may wrap the foil with a paper doily for a pretty presentation. Tie with ribbon.)

A Circle Basket   (AGES 6 AND UP)

Cut two 4-inch circles from pastel-colored posterboard. Fold each of the circles in half. Holding the half circles with the folds facing outward, place one folded circle inside the other. Slowly pull the

SONG ON A MAY MORNING

Hail, Bounteous May, that
*   doth inspire*
Mirth, and youth and
*   warm desire;*
Woods and grove are of
*   thy dressing,*
Hill and dale doth boast
*   thy blessing;*
Thus we salute thee with
*   our early song,*
And welcome thee, and
*   wish thee long.*

—JOHN MILTON

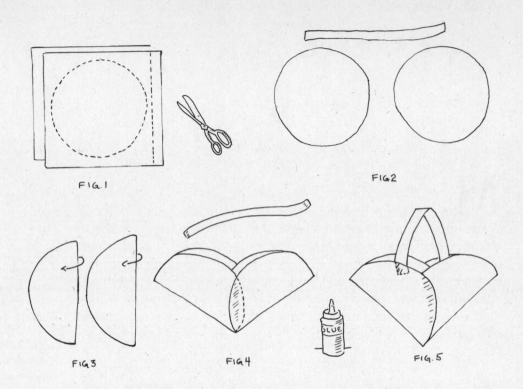

FIG.1   FIG.2   FIG.3   FIG.4   FIG.5

circles away from each other, until you have a point at the bottom. Glue together where the circles overlap. Cut an additional $1/2$- by 6-inch strip of paper for a handle and glue to the inside of the basket. Fill with treats.

City Watch

Check sidewalk flower vendors for spring blossoms. Ring neighborhood buzzers and leave friends May treats! Celebrate in the park afterward with ice cream and a dance around the Maypole! P.S. Be sure to wear your May crown!

A May Cone   (Ages 5 and Up)

Cut a 6-inch square out of colored or floral-printed paper. Turn the paper on its end, so corners face to the top, bottom, left, and right. Wrap the left-hand corner inside of the right-hand corner, forming a cone on the bottom and leaving a point at the top. Adjust so that the cone is tight at the bottom. Glue along the edge. (Secure with a loose rubber band or string until dry.) Punch holes on opposite sides and lace with a ribbon for a handle. Let the younger children help fill the cone with goodies.

A Maypole   (AGES 5 AND UP, WITH HELP)

No May Day celebration is complete without a Maypole to dance around or carry while a-Mayin'. Children can decorate the pole with fresh flowers or the tissue paper Fancy Flowers on page 89.

> *Posterboard (pastel colors are best)*
> *Two 12-inch round paper lace doilies*
> *Glue*
> *Scissors*
> *A hole punch*
> *Glue gun (optional)*
> *A thin wooden dowel*
> *Assorted curling ribbons in pastel shades*
> *Fresh or tissue paper flowers*

Cut a 12-inch circle out of the posterboard. (You can use a plate as a pattern if you want.) Glue a lace doily to each side of the circle. Punch holes along the perimeter of the circle with the hole puncher. Make a hole for the dowel in the center of the circle with the scissors. (Adults only, please.) Attach the dowel to the center of the circle with a bit of glue, and allow to dry thoroughly. (Adults may use a glue gun for this if they have one.) Cut the ribbon into various lengths and tie several strands through each hole around the edge of the circle. Curl the ends of the ribbons with the scissors (older kids can do this themselves using blunt scissors)—leaving some tightly curled while others are loose will give the best effect. Attach the flowers to the top of the circle—real flowers may be attached by poking thin wire through the circle; paper flowers may be glued in place. One child holds the Maypole aloft while the others dance around her.

May Crowns   (AGES 5, WITH HELP, TO ADULT)

May Day is the perfect spring day to make a crown of flowers for children to wear. Spring dandelions are traditional, though any flower with a sturdy 2- to 3-inch stem will do. The easiest method is to make a small slit in the stem with your finger, about 1 inch

Twist me a crown of
windflowers
That I may fly away . . .

—*CHRISTINA*
ROSSETTI

from the end. Thread the stem of the next flower through the slit and pull gently. (The head of the flower will prevent it from slipping through the hole.) Continue adding flowers until you have the length you want. Tie ends together with a pretty ribbon and a big bow. Place the May Crown on the child's head with the bow in the back.

Pussy Willow Kittens

The blossoming of pussy willows has announced the true arrival of spring for generations of children. According to an old Polish legend, pussy willows are really kittens. As the story goes, an old man was walking along a river bank with a sack of kittens. As he opened the bag and dumped the kittens into the river, the tall willow trees bent over and the kittens crawled onto the branches for safety!

Pussy Willow Kittens (AGES 4 AND UP)

Children long ago used to make spring pictures by gluing pussy willows to pieces of paper. Kids today can make similar pictures. Children can glue the pictures onto small folded cards to use as Thank-You notes or to give as gifts.

Construction paper
Pussy willow catkins
Glue
A felt tip pen

Glue several pussy willows to a piece of paper. Draw ears and a tail for each little kitten. Children long ago would draw them sitting on a fence with their tails hanging down. Have kids use their imaginations and fill in the background—my daughter has drawn a lone kitty sitting at a window looking at the moon.

We Cross the Stream

*We cross the stream where
    the willows weep,
Now laughter is in the air,
Along bare stems gray
    kittens peep,
Spring is everywhere!*

—HELEN MERRITT
RICHMOND

Simple Fun

Make Spring Catkins! Have children draw branches of pussy willows—provide kids with blue construction paper for the background, a gray or brown crayon for drawing the stem, and white chalk for making the catkins.

The Little "Spring" Gardener

Good Reading

Janet Wolf. *The Rosy Fat Magenta Radish*. Boston: Little, Brown, 1990. (Ages 3 to 6)

Spring is the perfect season to design a child's garden! Clear off a tabletop and provide graph paper, pencils, pens, a ruler, and a large stack of seed catalogues. Older children usually like to create their own gardens, whereas younger ones welcome a few suggestions. Keep in mind that some kids like neat and orderly rows, while others have a more haphazard approach—a tomato plant here, a lettuce plant there, two rows of radishes in the center, and a lone bean plant in the corner.

Following are some ideas for some theme gardens—a big hit with kids of all ages. Often a child's pet, favorite foods, or personality will lead the way in determining what sort of garden he would like to plant.

No matter which theme children choose, bring some whimsy into the design—children need to be able to *play* in their garden. (I parked an old Amish wheelbarrow in the midst of my daughter's garden. Often I would look up from my gardening chores to see her curled up inside, talking to herself or playing with one of our cats.) Old ladders can be sunk flat a few inches into the ground and used to house plants in individual cubbyholes. (This is great for mint, which has a tendency to wander!) Add trellises for height. Try making a living tipi. Kids will love using their tipi as a secret hideaway! (See our directions on page 99, for making one out of wooden dowels.) Paint a favorite saying or a line from a favorite poem on an old piece of wood for a garden decoration. Or try carving the child's name into a sign. (An adult or older sibling who loves woodworking could help with this project.) What child wouldn't be delighted to find a marker proclaiming this plot of land to be "Evan's Garden"!

MONSTERS!
OUTRAGEOUSLY
HUMONGOUS VARIETIES

Surrounded by these varieties, even adults will feel Lilliputian in size! Encourage several kids to try their hand with this garden design. Stage a neighborhood contest to see who can grow the largest vegetable in any or all categories. Better yet, suggest to kids that they enter their vegetables in the county fair, a local 4H chapter, or one of the world-class competitions. In addition to the pride and sense of accomplishment that they develop, it's a great way to earn some extra money. Try some of these hints to jump-start crops.

- Pick off all of the fruit appearing on the plant, except for two or three of the best looking ones. This ensures that those fruits remaining grow to a larger size.
- Sow seeds on a heap of manure or a compost pile.
- Give plants a drink of manure tea. Find some cow or horse manure (a few scoops or more) and put it in a bucket. Fill the bucket almost to the top with fresh water. Give plants a weekly drink of manure "tea," refilling bucket as necessary.

Some giant varieties kids may want to consider are:

- Basil—Mexican
- Carrot—Zino (world record holder at 7 pounds, 1½ ounces)
- Cucumber—Yard Long Armenian
- Radish—Crimson Long
- Summer Squash—Lagenaria
- Tomato—Oxheart Giantissimo

KID-SOURCE

The Cook's Garden
P.O. Box 535
Londonderry, VT 05148

Seeds Blum
Idaho City Stage
Boise, ID 83706

Nichols Garden Nursery
1190 North Pacific Highway
Albany, OR 97321

Simple Fun

Let kids make mosaics with leftover seeds. Provide paper, glue, and seeds. Try drawing the outline of a shape and letting children fill it in with assorted seeds.

SPRING

And buttercups are coming,
And scarlet columbine,
And in the sunny meadows
The Dandelions shine.

—*CELIA THAXTER*

The Teeny Tiny Garden

(AGES 3 AND UP,
WITH SUPERVISION)

This garden works well anywhere, but is particularly delightful for children who live in the city! Instead of planting seeds in the ground, keep them in individual containers. Pots can be grown in any sunny spot—especially window ledges or balconies. (Children should be closely supervised at great heights and have help in tending plants.)

"Baby" varieties, as they are commonly called, are specially bred to be picked as miniature vegetables. Growing their own baby veggies is a good way to get kids to eat their vegetables and a great way to bring a bit of "green" to a city home. Here are some petite choices.

- Basil—Fine Green, Piccolo Verde Fino
- Beet—Little Ball, Burpees Golden, Baby Beet Spinel
- Beans—Dandy, La Belle
- Carrots—Mokum, Minicor, Planet, Thumbelina, Sucram, Little Fingers and Sweetness (carrots benefit from adding a bit of clean sand to your soil)
- Corn—Tom Thumb, Baby Corn, Pretty Pops
- Cucumber—French Cornichons
- Eggplant—Slim Jim (great for container growing), Purple Pickling, Little Fingers
- Lettuce—Tom Thumb, Little Gem, Summer Baby Bib, Rubens Dwarf
- Onions—Early Aviv, Barletta
- Potato, New—Cherries Jubliee
- Peas—Petite Provencal, Precovil
- Pepper—Jingle Bells, Canapé
- Pumpkin—Jack Be Little, Munchkin
- Squash, Patty Pan—Sunburst Golden, Ronde de Nice, Sunburst Scallop, Peter Pan Scallop
- Tomato—Red Currant, Yellow Marble, Yellow Pear, Green Grape, Gold Nugget, Red Cherry, Ruby Pearl
- Turnip—de Milan, Tokyo Market
- Strawberries—Alpine
- Zucchini—Gold Rush

My Colorful Garden (AGES 3 AND UP, WITH SUPERVISION)

What could be more captivating to children than to plan a garden full of blue corn, brown peppers, and purple and white eggplant! Here are some unusually colorful vegetables to try.

- Beets—Golden Yellow, Albino White
- Beans—Dragon Tongue (gold with violet stripes)
- Carrots—Afghanistan (purple outside, yellow inside)
- Eggplant—Rosa Bianca
- Potato—All Blue (blue skin with lavender meat)
- Radish—Easter Egg (red, violet, lavender, and white)
- Tomato—Taxi (gold to orange)

A Wildlife Garden (AGES 3 AND UP, WITH SUPERVISION)

For children who want to attract animals to their yard, this garden will please. Plant snap beans, peas, soybeans, and peanuts for deer. Rabbits love all the legumes too, plus lettuce and pansies. Be sure to plant extra of everything—so they'll be plenty for all! For kids with pets, include some catnip for the kitty and some pennyroyal to chase the fleas from the dog. Add a row of sunflowers for the birds; Russian Mammoth at 10 to 12 feet tall is perfect in the back row. Don't forget to put a birdbath in the middle of the garden. (See page 111; of course, *this* one won't be "musical," since it won't be under a tree!)

A Living Tipi (ALL AGES)

Children love using their tipis as secret hideaways. Try climbing Malabar Spinach, or any of the vining peas. (Carouby de Maussane is a good choice—tall with lovely, edible flowers and pods.) Clear an area and stick six to eight 6-foot wooden dowels into the ground to form a circle. Bring them together at the top, and tie securely with gardening twine to form a tipi. Then push each dowel further into the ground to secure. Lace twine closely together in and out of the dowels, so the vine has a support to cling to. Make a shallow trench about 4 inches from the dowels around the out-

Simple Fun

Children love to check four o'clocks (*Mirabilis jalapa*) at four in the afternoon to see if the fragrant, trumpet-shaped flowers are actually open. Soak the large black seeds overnight before planting. Often four o'clocks have more than one color flower per plant!

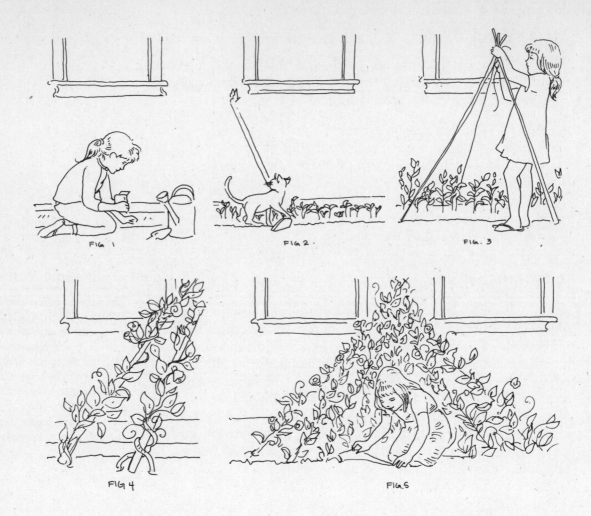

FIG 1

FIG 2

FIG. 3

FIG 4

FIG 5

side perimeter, and plant your seeds according to the directions on the packet. Kids will love checking on the seedlings' progress, and helping the new tendrils wind around the twine. Remember to clear a small entrance to the hideaway so children can enter easily!

Starting Your Seeds   (All Ages)

Children enjoy planting seeds in containers and can get a jump-start on the growing season as well. Protect the work area by putting down several layers of newspaper, and gather the following supplies:

> *Assorted containers—egg cartons, milk cartons, aluminum pans, plastic*
> *   food containers*
> *Wooden markers (popsicle sticks work well)*
> *Waterproof pen*
> *Potting mixture*
> *Seed packets*
> *Plant mister*
> *Clear plastic tray covers (optional)*
> *Pepper shaker*
> *Tweezers for sowing seeds (optional)*

Poke holes in the bottom of the containers so the water can drain properly. Label the wooden markers for each type of seed. Fill the containers with the potting mixture up to about $1/2$ inch from the top. Wet the mixture thoroughly—the easiest method is to use the sprayer at the sink or to place under gently running water. Allow containers to drain. Choose a packet of seeds and sow the desired amount in each container using a pepper shaker, tweezers, or by taking a pinch of seeds and sprinkling carefully. Cover the seeds lightly with additional potting mixture to a depth of three times the size of the seed. (Refer to instructions on individual packets for those varieties that need light to germinate.)

Moisten the seeds lightly with a plant mister and add the markers. Set the containers in a warm spot to germinate, covering seeds with a clear plastic tray, if desired. Children love to check their seeds daily. Do not allow seeds to dry out. At the first signs of life, remove the cover, and place in a sunny location or under fluorescent lights. Promote healthy growth by removing weak or undersized seedlings.

Simple Fun

Buttercups (*Ranunculus*) are for butter lovers! Find out if your friend loves butter with this old-time flower. Hold a blossom under her chin and ask, "Do you love butter?" (A yellow glow will appear there if she does, according to tradition!) Look for the Turban variety for the showiest blooms.

My Garden Notebook   (AGES 5 AND UP)

Kids love to keep a record of their plants' progress. Purchase an inexpensive ring binder and have children create a page for every type of seedling they start. Write the name of the plant and a sentence or two about its growth every day or week, or however often

Simple Fun

Daisy (*Bellis perennis*) Fortunes! Long ago, young girls would pick a fistful of grass with their eyes closed. However many daisies were in the bunch would represent the number of years before they would marry. Children today still play "He loves me, he loves me not . . ."

Simple Fun

Hollyhock (*Althaea rosea*) dolls are an old-fashioned favorite! Place the stem of an opened flower (the body) into the base of a bud (the head). Tie a piece of ribbon around to secure. This statuesque beauty is a favorite of bumblebees and hummingbirds too!

your child wants to. Add a picture of the full-grown plant from a seed catalogue, an extra seed if you have one, the date started, and so on.

Favorite Childhood Flowers

Certain flowers in the plant world are especially interesting to kids, captivating them for various reasons. Whether dazzling in color, quick to grow (thus giving prompt satisfaction!), or heady with perfume, particular plants become childhood favorites.

Chinese Lanterns (*Physalis alkekengi*)

What child could resist these papery, bobbing, bright orange globes! This sun lover is a hardy soul and can quite easily take over a corner of the garden. Wonderful for party decorations (see page 137) or as an addition to a dried flower arrangement.

Honesty (*Lunaria annua*)

Also known as the money plant. Sow in a shady spot during the month of June. When the plant matures, cut the stalks and hang in a cool spot until dried. A must in any Fairy Garden, honesty is also fun to use as play money, tokens, or dishes for a doll's tea party.

Lady's Mantle (*Alchemilla mollis*)

My own personal favorite, and a must in any child's garden. This lovely plant with fringed leaves delicately touched with pink can grow in half-shade. Children love to check the plant first thing in the morning—each leaf has a drop of dew in its center.

Sunflower (*Helianthus annus*)

True happiness itself! The taller varieties are perfect for the back row of the garden. Leftover heads make wonderful ready-made bird feeders.

Bachelor's Button (*Centaurea cyanus*)

Also known as the cornflower, this favorite brings a welcome shade of blue to the garden. Long ago, young men in England would carry these blooms in their pockets to predict the outcome of their love interests—if the flower lived they would marry their current love, if the flower died they would find a new love.

Nasturtium (*Tropaeolum majus*)

These peppery delights are perfect at the entrance to a child's secret hideaway. Ranging in color from yellow, to orange, and red—both the flowers and the leaves are edible. Trailing varieties are wonderful in hanging baskets, and they attract hummingbirds as well.

Johnny Jump Up (*Viola tricolor*)

Charming, dainty little flowers with whimsical faces. Many years ago this little flower was thought to predict the future—four lines for hope, five lines for hope from fear, seven lines for everlasting love, eight lines for erratic in nature, nine for a change of heart, and eleven for no luck in matters of the heart.

Sweet Pea (*Lathyrus odoratus*)

Deliciously scented and available in an endless array of colors. Soak the tough seed overnight. Beautiful as a living tipi or growing on any upright support.

Snapdragon (*Antirrhinum majus*)

Children are drawn to the beastlike looks of this classic childhood flower. Blooms endlessly from spring to autumn. Kids can hide tiny rolled-up secret messages inside the blooms!

Obedient Plant (*Physostegia virginiana*)

This blossom has a ball-bearing feature and can be bent into several positions indefinitely—facing to the front, back, or to one side.

Lamb's Ear (*Stachys lanata*)

The woolly, silvery-white leaves of this plant were once used as bandages due to their downy texture. Children will love nursing

QUEEN ANNE'S LACE (*DAUCUS CAROTA*)

A closer look explains the origin of this charmer's name. The large, flat white head is actually made up of dozens of tiny delicate flowers, and quite similar to a small piece of delicately worked lace.

QUEEN ANNE, QUEEN ANNE

Queen Anne, Queen Anne,
* has washed her lace*
(She chose a summer day)
And hung it in a grassy place
To whiten, if it may.
Queen Anne, Queen Anne,
* has left it there,*
And slept the dewy night;
Then waked, to find the
* sunshine fair,*
And all the meadows white . . .

—*MARY LESLIE NEWTON*

Name that plant! Water-proof pens and paint are all kids need to make fun garden markers. Write the plant's name on the marker in fancy letters (you can use a paint stirrer), or draw a picture.

Simple Fun

Make a Care File. Older kids can write instructions for watering and fertilizing their plants on individual 3-by 5-inch cards. Print the name of the plant and add a picture or drawing for easy reference. Arrange alphabetically in a card file.

their favorite stuffed animals and dolls back to health as they wrap their limbs in the soft leaves. A wonderful ground cover in poor, scraggly soil.

Gardening Tips

There are some wonderful children's gardening books on the market today to get kids started. Here are some key points to consider before planning a child's garden:

- Locate the garden where an adult can keep a watchful eye on the kids. Gardens that can be seen from a kitchen window, family room, or porch will give grownups greater peace of mind.
- Choose a suitable site. (Near the house is a good idea for younger ones, due to those hurried trips to the bathroom.) Make sure the location doesn't interfere with the root system of any trees or bushes and gets at least six hours of full sun or choose a shady spot for growing shade-loving varieties of plants.
- Once a site has been established, scratch the plot dimensions in the dirt with a stick. Many garden designers suggest starting with a space no larger than 3 by 6 feet. Remove all large rocks and weeds, and enrich the soil if necessary. Most soils benefit from a layer of compost, aged manure, and a sprinkling of lime. Have the soil tested for maximum results—contact your local county agricultural extension service for more information.
- Perhaps most important—start small. Gardening catalogues can be hard to resist for a child, with page after page of luscious fruits, vegetables, and flowers. Begin with a few proven first-time winners: beans, peas, corn, nasturtiums, and sunflowers. The seeds are large, and the results are usually pretty foolproof.
- Purchase kids a set of their own child-size gardening tools. Learning proper use and care of gardening tools is important at this stage. Have children practice the four major tasks involved in gardening with tools: digging, raking, weeding, and hoeing. A beginner's collection of tools might include a spade, rake, hoe, fork, trowel, scissors, raffia (for tying plants), wooden markers, and a waterproof pen. Let kids use an old basket or container to store all their smaller gardening supplies. A small

wheelbarrow or watering can would make a wonderful gift for a junior gardener.

• Encouragement and praise are essential in fostering a lifelong love of gardening. Even if that spindly tomato plant only yields one or two tomatoes, make a fuss over the achievement!

• "Harden off" seedlings before transplanting to their new home. Kids can water plants a bit less frequently for a few days beforehand. Begin sunlight exposure with a few hours on an overcast morning, and gradually build up to a full day in filtered sun. Let kids place plants on trays, baking dishes, and in cardboard boxes for ease in transporting.

• Children are proud of their gardening accomplishments. Before transplanting, suggest tying a ribbon around a few containers and giving them away as gifts.

Good Bugs   (AGES 3 AND UP, WITH SUPERVISION)

Not all bugs are harmful to plants. One of my children's favorite gardening activities is releasing their "good bugs" into the garden to combat the harmful effects of the "bad bugs."

Ladybugs

It's best to release these childhood friends at dusk so they are less likely to fly off. These "good bugs" and their larvae can eat several times their weight in aphids, mealy bugs, and other harmful insects daily. Allow children to spray the ladybugs lightly with a mister before releasing them from the container.

Praying Mantis

Egg cases can be ordered by mail. Usually two to three cases is enough to establish a colony. They can be fun to hatch, though adult supervision is a must! Keep the cases in the refrigerator until warm weather has arrived (usually the end of April or the beginning of May), then bring to room temperature, and place in a glass jar. Make a heavy paper lid: punch a few small holes, with a sewing needle, in the paper and carefully tape it to the top of the jar. The insects will make a slit in the side of the egg case and will emerge in a short while. Place in the garden within twenty-four hours.

KID-SOURCE

Smith and Hawken
Arbor Lane, Box 6900
Florence, KY 41022
800-776-3336
Extensive catalogue featuring kids' tools, gloves, books, seeds collections, and a Children's Gardening Kit.

Brooklyn Botanical Garden
1000 Washington Avenue
Brooklyn, NY 11225
718-622-4433
Discovery Center and Workshops for families, composting, worm bin demonstration center, children's garden, hands-on activities.

National Gardening Association
180 Flynn Avenue
Burlington, VT 05401
802-863-1308
Extensive information on gardening with kids. Books, workshops, and a Growlab—an indoor lab for classroom use.

W. Atlee Burpee, Co.
300 Park Avenue
Warminster, PA 18974
215-674-4900
Offers a "Kinder-Garden" with seeds, markers, and growing instructions.

KID-SOURCE

Beneficial insects can be ordered from:
Peaceful Valley Farm Supply
110 Spring Hill Drive
Grass Valley, CA 95945
916-272-4769
Free catalogue with children's section. Mail-order ladybugs and praying mantises with complete release instructions included.

Simple Fun

Children can share some of their worms with fellow gardeners. Let friends "adopt" handfuls of worms. They and their gardens will be thankful!

KID-SOURCE

Kids can order worms, worm bins, and books from the following source:
Flowerfield Enterprise
10332 Shaver Road
Kalamazoo, MI 49002
616-327-0108
Mary Appelhoff has written two books of interest to children. *Worms Eat My Garbage* and *Worms Eat Our Garbage: Classroom Activities for a Better Environment*. Both are available by mail.

The Earthworm Ranch (AGES 5 AND UP)

Another friend to the junior gardener is the earthworm. These wiggly little creatures make tunnels through the soil, allowing air and water to get to the roots of the plants, besides producing rich castings that are a good source of nutrients for the garden.

Kids can make an Earthworm Ranch from an old wooden box or build one out of plywood with an adult's help. Place a thick layer of soil, compost, and/or decayed leaves in the bottom of the box and have kids add their worms. Children must check the soil often to keep it moist, as earthworms like a humid environment. Cover the top of the box with a thin piece of plywood or a square of black plastic to simulate the worms' dark underground habitat. Earthworms love weekly leftovers from the kitchen—especially veggies, pasta, and bread. In about two months, the worms will have consumed the goodies left for them and turned them into rich castings, which are pure gold for the garden. These should be scattered in the garden. Turn on the hose and carefully wet down the garden to allow the nutrients to seep into the soil.

If the children lose interest in feeding the worms, be sure to have them place the worms in the soil so they may continue to do their good work. Rough up the soil so they can easily "dig in." Keep the worms out of direct sun. Gently sprinkle a thin layer of soil over them and keep it moist.

More Fun with Worms

• Help children set up a weekly chart—the worms should be gently turned every 5 to 7 days, and the castings scattered into the garden. Let kids turn the hose on in the garden afterward. The nutrients will seep down to the plants' root systems more efficiently after a nice long drink.

City Kids Go Green

For children who live in cities, apartment buildings, or who are without a yard of your own to dig in, these gardens are especially for you! (Though any kids who want to "get growing" will want to try them too.)

City Watch

Set up a community garden. Kids and adults working together can take back empty lots and abandoned plots and bring them alive with flowers, vegetables, butterflies, and other living creatures! Contact American Community Gardening Association, 325 Walnut Street, Philadelphia, PA 19106 for more information.

Highwire Plants
(AGES 4 AND UP, WITH HELP)

When short on ground or shelf space kids can look up—and hang their garden! Garden centers offer many types of hanging containers, though inventive growers can construct a few of their own. Old kitchen colanders, three-tiered wire baskets, and salad spinner "inserts" all work well for those with a little outside space to hang them. For inside gardeners, there are hanging pots with drip protectors at gardening or hardware stores. To prepare containers, first line them with sphagnum moss, available at garden centers. Line the bottom with about 2 inches of moss, and the sides with about 1 inch. (Kids will find it easier to soak the moss with water first, before handling.) Fill the prepared container with potting soil. Soils are available ready-mixed or kids can prepare their own mixtures. One part soil to two parts vermiculite works well. (Some gardeners like to add perlite or peat moss to their recipes, to lighten the soil.)

Make holes in the soil for the plants. Try putting the tallest plant in the center, and the smaller or cascading ones at the edge. Place the plants in the holes and press the soil gently around the roots. Kids can hang their gardens by making a tipi out of wire. Cut four 14-inch pieces of medium-weight wire and twist them together at one end to form a hook. Attach each of the other ends to the container, evenly spacing them around the edge. (Adults should make sure the wires are attached securely, as the containers will be quite heavy after watering.)

Adults can help children hang their garden in full sun for those plants that require lots of sunshine or in a sheltered spot for those that prefer shade to partial shade. Most plants come with markers listing their preferences, or kids can look up the information in a gardening book.

Highwire Plants should be checked often to make sure that the soil is moist. Kids can water their gardens with a hose turned to the fine mist setting or with a long-nosed watering can. Remind kids to remove any dead blossoms or leaves from time to time to ensure proper growth and continuous bloom on flowering plants. Plants should be fertilized regularly as well. Plants respond to love and can become a child's "good friend" for many years to come with proper care.

Green Windowsills (ALL AGES)

Herbs or small flowering plants can transform a child's windowsill into a living oasis. Many kitchens have sunny windows that can be homes for tasty treats. Kids will love to add pinches of herbs to their favorite dishes.

Parsley is easy to grow but a slow starter. Soak seeds in water for two days before planting to speed things up. (Kids may be better off buying a seedling.) Coriander is yummy in homemade salsa. Since this plant doesn't like to change homes once it is planted, kids should pick out a medium-size container and avoid repotting. Partial shade is okay. Pots of cheery, yellow marigolds are a welcome addition to a child's bedroom. Have children check local garden centers for small pots of herbs or flowering plants.

My Silly, Upside Down Plant! (AGES 5 AND UP, WITH HELP)

Children can grow a hanging plant from a carrot or a beet—though not in the usual sense! In this case the vegetable itself becomes the hanging basket. Have kids pick a nice, fat vegetable with leaves. Cut the leaves off of the end, leaving about a half inch of stem remaining. Slice the bottom part of the vegetable off (adults only) so that there is about a 1-inch piece left. Using the tip of a sharp paring knife (adults again), scoop out the inside of the vegetable to create a little "bowl." Stick four toothpicks at intervals around the side of the vegetable and turn it so that the stem end is pointing down. Tie a length of yarn to each toothpick and knot all of them together at the end. Kids now have a "hanging plant" with a built-in watering cup! Kept full of water, their vegetable will soon sprout leaves —upside down!

A Terrarium (ALL AGES, WITH HELP)

To a child, growing plants in a terrarium is like having a small world within a world! And with the moisture trapped inside the container, kids don't have to water as often. You'll need a large-mouthed container (glass or clear plastic so children can view their garden) with a lid. Fill the bottom with a 1-inch layer of small stones for drainage. Add a thin layer of crushed charcoal (available

Good Reading

Barbara A. Huff. *Greening the City Streets: The Story of Community Gardens.* N.Y.: Clarion Books, 1990. (Ages 6 and up)

City Watch

Plant a "sidewalk garden" at the base of a tree on your block! (Get permission from your superintendent first.) Edge plants with large rocks or bricks for added protection.

Good Reading

Giulio Maestro. *The Remarkable Plant in Apartment 4*. N.Y.: Bradbury Press, 1973. (Ages 4 to 10)

at garden or aquarium-supply stores) to prevent the growth of fungi. Lay a piece of fine-mesh screening or nylon stocking on top of the charcoal to prevent soil from leaching into the drainage layer. Top with a layer of soil. Make holes in the soil with the end of a long wooden spoon, and carefully position the plants. Using the spoon, have children gently tamp the soil around the base of each plant. (Plants should not be crowded to ensure proper air circulation.) Garden centers can suggest plants that do well in terrariums, though the following make good choices: miniature ferns, English ivy, philodendron, strawberry begonia, evergreen seedlings, and violets. Kids can collect assorted items to add to their plant-scape such as: moss, lichen-covered pieces of wood, tiny pinecones, attractive stones, shells, and nicely shaped twigs or bark. Ceramic frogs and lizards add a whimsical touch. Once all the plant material is in place children should water lightly. Place the top on the container and put in a well-lit room, out of direct sunlight. Once established, terrariums need little maintenance. Children can water lightly about once a month with tepid water—plant misters, small-bulb syringes, and salt shakers filled with water work well. (Have kids mark the calendar each month, as a reminder.) Dead leaves or flowers can be removed with a small pair of scissors. If condensation should appear on the inside of the container, leave the lid slightly ajar until the moisture has dried up, then replace lid as before.

The Crystal Garden   (AGES 6 AND UP, WITH SUPERVISION)

Not all gardens involve the use of plant material! Place chunks of charcoal, brick, or earthenware in a large glass container. Add a few old sponges too. Dampen with a plant mister. Combine 6 tablespoons of laundry bluing,* 6 tablespoons of ammonia, and 6 tablespoons of water in a small container and pour over the "rocks." (Adults or older children should do this step.) Have kids sprinkle a few drops of food coloring over the top, followed by 6 tablespoons of common salt. Let stand for a few hours, until crystals start to form. The garden can then be moved to a special spot where children can watch the magical transformation!

*Bluing can be purchased by mail from Mrs. Stewart's Bluing, P.O. Box 201405, Bloomington, MN 55420.

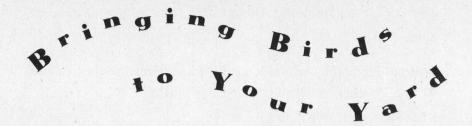

Bringing Birds to Your Yard

Spring is a time of bustling activity in the bird world. This is the season for building nests, laying eggs, and feeding young. Children can attract birds to their yards by setting up a friendly environment. By providing food, bathing facilities, and shelter of some kind they can help birds feel right at home. Robins and bluebirds are some of the earliest arrivals this time of year. They don't travel that far south in the winter and are first on the scene come spring.

Favorite Foods (AGES 3 AND UP, WITH SUPERVISION)

Just like kids, certain types of birds love some foods more than others! The quickest way to get birds to come close is by providing the food that they like to eat. Kids should note that every time they add an additional type of food, they will attract another species of bird.

Chickadees, red-bellied woodpeckers, nuthatches, blue jays, warblers, titmice:

Seeds mixed with peanut butter, lard, bacon grease, or meat drippings.

Mockingbirds, orioles, scarlet tanagers:

Orange halves, apple cores, and pinecones studded with raisins.

Yellow goldfinch:

Black thistle seed.

Simple Fun

Make a "Musical" Birdbath! Add some rocks to a shallow container so birds can "perch" while drinking. Fill with 3 inches of water and place it under a tree. Suspend a plastic jug filled with water from a branch overhead. Poke a small hole in the bottom so the water drips slowly into the birdbath. Birds will be attracted by the sound!

RECYCLE FOR THE BIRDS

Kids can write away for this free brochure and learn how to recycle everyday containers into birdfeeders! The National Wildlife Federation, 8925 Leesburg Pike, Vienna, VA 22184.

Cardinals, goldfinch, chickadees, blue jays, nuthatches, evening grosbeak, purple finches, grackles, tufted titmice, mourning doves:

Sunflower seeds.

Redwing blackbirds, bobwhite, cardinals, catbirds, mourning doves, purple finches, grackles, pigeons, sparrows, starlings:

Cracked corn, millet, and doughnuts.

Blue jays, cardinals, doves, grackles, sparrows, starlings:

White millet, red millet, wheat, and sunflower seeds.

Kids can also plant some bushes or trees that offer birds a favorite food source. In addition to being a tasty treat, the plants will provide shelter from bad weather and predators and just may prove to be the perfect spot for a nest.

Robins, mockingbirds, evening grosbeaks, blue jays, chickadees, catbirds:

Mulberry trees.

Bluebirds, cardinals, cedar waxwings, purple finches, robins, sparrows:

Holly, pyracantha, or red cedar.

Note: *Blueberries, blackberries, and raspberries are a favorite treat of most birds. And, whatever the birds don't eat, kids can enjoy themselves!*

Peanut Butter Delight

(AGES 3 AND UP, WITH SUPERVISION)

Kids can have fun making their own homemade birdseed treats. Many of the ingredients for this birdseed recipe are common household ingredients found in most kitchens.

> *2 cups fat (meat drippings, bacon fat, or lard)*
> *1 cup peanut butter*

Melt the fat and add it to the peanut butter. Stir to combine well. Add any or all of the following ingredients: crushed eggshell, cornflakes, cornmeal, oatmeal, apple chunks, currants, raisins, crushed dry dog food, or powdered skim milk. Place the mixture in a cardboard milk or juice container and refrigerate until it's firm, then peel down the carton sides and slice as needed. (This mixture may be stuffed into pinecones or made in individual paper cups and hung in a plastic mesh bag available in the produce section of your grocery store.)

A Bird Cafe   (AGES 5 AND UP, WITH HELP)

Children can turn a cardboard or plastic milk container into a simple feeder. Cut away one side of the container, leaving about 2 inches at the bottom for a perch. Poke two holes in the bottom of the feeder and thread a 1-foot-long, 1/4-inch-diameter round dowel through the holes. Punch a hole in the top of the feeder and lace with a piece of twine or wire for hanging.

Some kids like to put their feeders on a pulley system so they can move them closer to the window each time they add food. Birds are cautious creatures, though, so suggest that children hang their feeders in a sheltered area. Try hanging more than one feeder, if there is room. When one station is busy, smaller birds will go to the remaining ones. If squirrels tend to "take over" the feeder, try giving them their own ground-floor restaurant—fill a shallow tray with nuts, corn, and apple cores. Kids can now sit back and enjoy the show!

I Spy   (AGES 5 AND UP)

With the flurry of feathers that spring brings, a child will want to keep track of the activity in her own bird watcher's journal. Early morning and late afternoons tend to be the busiest feeding times for birds. Encourage your child to write down her observations: the date, species of bird seen, how many birds there were, what they were doing, and their food preferences. (Some birds will swoop in by the dozens, like starlings. Others, like the blue jay, will make a mess when they eat.) Note which birds build a nest and where, and what type of building materials were used, when the first "peeps" from baby birds were heard, and when they left the nest.

Good Reading

• Judy Pederson. *The Tiny Patient*. N.Y.: Alfred A. Knopf, 1989. (Ages 4 to 8)
• Barbara Bash. *Urban Roosts: Where Birds Nest in the City*. Boston: Little, Brown, 1990. (Ages 6 to 10)

Simple Fun

About a week after kids have made a Bird-nest Buddy, take a spring walk and check the yard and neighborhood for any rainbow-colored nests!

Build a Bird-nest Buddy   (AGES 3 AND UP)

Children can help the birds in their neighborhood build their nests come May or June by offering them an assortment of nesting materials. Kids delight in spotting the brightly colored strips of cloth or paper that they have provided, and will enjoy pointing out the nests that they "helped" build.

Mesh bag (onion sacks from the grocery work well)
Assorted pieces of colorful cloth, paper, ribbon, yarn, string, and thread

Stuff all of the nesting material into the mesh bag. Pull some of the ends out of the bag, so it is easier for the birds to get. Find a tree with lots of branches, and hang the bag up out of the reach of any neighborhood cats. A location visible from a window will allow children to watch the birds as they swoop down and carry off bits of material. Nest building is a huge project often requiring more than 100 trips for just one nest!

Note: *Kids can also pull a coat hanger into a diamond shape and slide the mesh bag over it. Weave the loose scraps through the holes.*

City Search:
An Architectural Exploration

(AGES 6 AND UP)

Kids want to be outside this time of year! What better way to capture their interest than with an Architectural Exploration. Whether they are city kids longing to be out of doors from apartment buildings and brownstones, or country kids longing for an adventure in the city, a trek through the streets in search of design and construction elements can be just the answer.

Except for budding architects or draftspeople, most kids can benefit from a trip to their local library first. They can familiarize themselves with the terminology of the various architectural elements and learn some interesting facts as well. Example: What are gargoyles? Are they purely decorative accents, or do they have a purpose? (They are actually waterspouts in the shape of fascinating creatures.)

Have children draw up a list of architectural elements to look for and cross them off as they find them. Kids may want to form teams and see who finds the most items in a given period of time. If so, be sure to decide what the boundaries are, and set a time limit. One half hour is a good start for the first exploration.

A sample list of architectural elements might look like this:

A building made of brick
A building made of stone
A building made of concrete
A building made of glass
A building made of wood
A building with double front doors
A building with a porch

KID-SOURCE

Kids can write for an architectural information packet by sending $2.50 to The Center for Understanding the Built Environment, 5328 West 67th Street, Prairie Village, KS 66208.

A fountain
A piece of garden statuary
A stained glass window or door
A bay window
A dormer window
A revolving door
Arches
Latticework
A gate
Gargoyles

Ionic columns
Doric columns
A chimney
A smokestack

Note: *Adjust the list to the neighborhood. Country kids, or city kids visiting rural areas, can play the game by changing the list of elements to look for. A rural list could include: a front porch, a back porch, a silo. (This is a fun way to get to know a new city or town while traveling. Who knows what kids may discover around the next corner!)*

Good Reading

• David Macalay. *City.* N.Y.: Houghton Mifflin, 1983. (Ages 10 and up)
• Jane D'Alelio. *I Know That Building! Discovering Architecture with Activities and Games.* Washington, D.C.: Preservation Press, 1989. (Ages 7 and up)

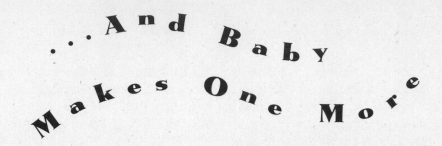

...And Baby Makes One More

(ALL AGES)

Spring being the season of new beginnings, we thought it the appropriate time of year to highlight some Sibling Fun! The arrival of a new baby can be very stressful for some children. The following activities can help ease the way and make the addition of a new family member a joyful one.

MY BROTHER
_____

Brothers and sisters,
Best of friends.
The love between them
never ends . . .

—*LAUREN WINSLOW*
BARTA (AGE 7)

• Before the arrival of the baby have each sibling make his or her very own "Baby Album." Gather together a few photographs from each child's first year. Look at these pictures together. Kids love looking at photos of themselves as babies, and the album can be a great springboard for conversation with them about the new arrival.

• When shopping for all of those baby necessities, let siblings help pick out items. Let them use a few of the items on their own dolls or stuffed animals. Kids love to copy adults and will enjoy changing diapers and burping their own "babies."

• Make a "Big Brother" or "Big Sister" kit and let the sibling join in with the care of the new family member. Suggested items might include a baby brush, small stuffed animals, rattles, or a tape of lullabies to listen to together.

• Kids will take great pride in making something special for the new baby. Suggest a drawing, mobile, or picture frame.

• Children can learn some new finger games and "tickling rhymes" to share with the baby. Check the local library for books of rhymes.

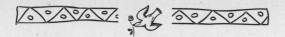

Have a Spring Fling!

Following are a few simple outdoor activities to help children get the best out of this season. All are proven winners that will bring hours of pleasure to the kids in your life—and get them started on their Spring Flings!

Tin Can Walkers (Ages 4 and Up, with Help)

My children use these to walk through spring puddles! Kids can decorate the cans with colorful strips of adhesive tape and adhesive stickers—check your local hardware, novelty, and office-supply stores.

> *2 jumbo tin cans*
> *Can openers (the punch type that makes a triangular hole)*
> *Two 5-foot lengths of rope*
> *Decorative tape and stickers (optional)*

Remove the top of the can with a can opener. Rinse and dry the can. Place each can on your work surface with the open end down. Punch two holes opposite each other in the sides of the can, right below the rim (do this on the end that is not open). Thread one length of rope through the holes and tie the ends of the rope together in a secure knot. The knotted end of the rope should be inside the can. Do the same with the other can. Have kids practice

walking—place one foot on the top of each can and hold the loop of rope in your hand. (Ropes may need to be adjusted for each child.) Take normal steps—you're walking on stilts!

Hop to the Finish! (ALL AGES)

Children can create colorful birds and challenge each other to a spring race. This is an old-fashioned outdoor amusement sure to bring whoops and cheers to your crowd. All it takes is paper and string—within a few minutes kids will be at the starting line, raring to go!

Lightweight cardboard or posterboard (the kind that comes in new shirts is ideal)
Pencil
Scissors
12 feet of string or dental floss
Crayons, markers, colored pencils (optional)

Have children trace a 5½- to 6½-inch circle on the cardboard. (A plate makes a good pattern.) Make the circle into a bird by drawing a head, two wings and a tail. Cut the bird out and color it, if desired. Make a hole for the string; it should be about 1½ inches below the top of the circle. Cut the string into a 10- to 12-foot length. Tie one end of the string to the bottom rung of a lawn chair and thread the other end through the hole in the bird. Hold the string taut and place the bird 12 inches from the beginning of the string. (Bird should be standing on its tail to start the race.) Make the bird hop by releasing the string and pulling it taut again. (Every time you pull the string taut the bird will stand. Whenever the string is released slightly the bird will flop either forward or backward.) Pull and release until the bird has reached the other end of the string. (Now for the real challenge!) Pull and release and make the bird hop back to you. The first bird home is the winner. (Younger children will find it easier to simply reach the chair.) Toddlers love to wiggle the string and watch the birds dance!

Note: *Older kids and adults will achieve a degree of skill with practice —balancing the bird on its tail and pulling and releasing so that the bird "tail walks" home!*

This activity adapts beautifully to holidays and birthday parties—cut the paper out in different symbols for each occasion. Try Christmas trees for Christmas, blue stars for Hanukkah, and giant firecrackers for the Fourth of July! Birthday cakes with candles work well for parties and are a great way to entertain the kids.

Simple Fun

Check out the action below the water's surface with an "Underwater Viewer." Remove both ends from a large tin can. Cover one end with plastic wrap, and secure with a giant rubber band. Submerge covered end in water and place face up to can. Look for tadpoles, water-walkers, and other spring creatures in your local pond!

Kazoo Kids   (ALL AGES)

Nothing heralds the arrival of spring like a song! Kids can fill the air with springtime melodies as they hum some favorite tunes.

A cardboard tube (from paper towels, tinfoil, etc.)
Waxed paper
Scissors
Rubber bands

Cut a piece of waxed paper large enough to cover one end of the roll and come up the sides about an inch. Place the waxed paper over one end of the tube and secure with several twists of a rubber band. Make a hole on one side of the tube about $1^1/2$ inches from the covered end. Have child place the open end of the tube up to her mouth and sing. (The easiest way to get that "kazoo" sound is to sing "dee-dee-dee." Just make sure the child's mouth is completely in the tube to get the right effect.)

MUD FUN

Making mud pies has to be the quintessential springtime activity of childhood. As the snow of winter melts, the earth turns to mud—a true bane to most adults, though sheer delight to children. Rather than cautioning the kids to "stay out of the mud," why not dress them in their oldest clothes and arm them with spoons, cups, buckets, and pie tins and let them go right into the midst of it! This to me is what being young is all about. And to those adults who would like to relive their days of youth—I urge you to join them!

Mud Pies   (ALL AGES, WITH SUPERVISION)

There is a certain knack to making proper mud pies—the batter must be of just the right consistency. Dump some mud in a container and experiment by adding a bit of water at a time. Once the dough seems right, turn it into a cake or pie tin, decorate, and set in the sun to bake. Look for small blossoms, flowers, twigs, leaves and seed pods to place on top. Children can also make doughnuts and cookies. For cupcakes, line muffin tin with paper liners and fill with mud batter. Bake in the sun until firm. Children love peeling the paper liners off and pretending to eat them!

An Edible Mud Pie

When kids have an urge for something to eat after their play in the mud—surprise them with a pie of their own!

¹/₃ cup melted butter
1¹/₂ cups chocolate or chocolate chip cookies, finely crushed
2 quarts chocolate ice cream, softened
1 cup fudge topping
Additional cookies for decoration (optional)
Whipped cream (optional)

Melt the butter over low heat. Crush the cookies in a blender, and combine well with the melted butter. Press the mixture into the bottom and sides of a 9-inch deep dish pie pan. Place in the freezer for about 1 hour, or until firm. Spread half of the ice cream over the pie shell. Add a layer of half of the fudge topping, and the remaining ice cream. Top with the remaining fudge topping and cookies. Freeze for about 4 hours, or until firm. Serve plain or with whipped cream.

KID-SOURCE

Hearthsong
800-325-2502
Free catalogue. Seasonal and Holiday supplies, books, toys.

Duncraft
102 Fisherbille Road
Penacook, NH 03303
800-252-5696
Wild bird supplies. A Child's First Birdfeeder Kit; Window feeders, etc., for city dwellers.

Big City Kite Company
1210 Lexington Avenue
New York, NY 10028
212-472-2623
Classic source for kites. Price list; mail order too.

Maid of Scandinavia
32-44 Raleigh Avenue
Minneapolis, MN 55416
800-328-6722
The ultimate baking and candy-making catalogue.

The Signs

Keep an eye out for these earthly changes!

A NIGHT FOR STARGAZING

With a Star Machine kids can beam the constellations on their ceiling and get to know our stellar neighbors! Check your vision with our Big Dipper test, locate the North Star, and make a Star Tracking Book to record your findings.

MIDSUMMER'S EVE

Honor the summer solstice with a solar trick—the Sun's Fade Out. Make lacy paper Lanterns, a fairy wand, and a Wacky Cake with Buttercream Frosting for a Fairy's Tea Party! Fill in the blanks of a Fairy's Tale and create your own silly story!

THE FOURTH OF JULY

Celebrate America's birthday with a Quill Pen—just like they used in the 1700s! Make up a batch of Blueberry Ink and decorate a Holiday Drum for your own parade.

BACKYARD WATER FUN

Stay cool on even the hottest summer day with a Water Snake, Ultimate Slide, and some Water Balloons. Mix up a batch of bubble mix and step inside a Giant Bubble! A host of Icy Cold Treats for kids to whip up.

FIREFLIES

Thrill kids on a summer night with a Firefly Lamp! See how fireflies react to temperature changes with the Warm Water Trick; learn how to call fireflies closer with a flashlight. Play "Firefly" with a friend!

SUMMER STRAWBERRIES

Fragrant, red, and juicy—let the sun cook you up a batch of Sunshine Strawberry Preserves! Try the ultimate summer dessert: Strawberry Shortcake.

SHADY CHARACTERS

Keep cool with An Easy Newspaper Topper or an Ultimate Summer Brim! Fashion the best hat on the block with More Lids for the Kids.

THE LITTLE "SUMMER" GARDENER

Kids will eat all their veggies with Hunter's Cheese Sauce on top! Surprise kids with their name in "plants"—with That's My Name! Grow a giant pumpkin in the Great Pumpkin Contest.

# of Summer

CALLING ALL BUTTERFLIES!

Plant these Favorite Blooms and you'll be covered up with butterflies! Learn the difference between Butterflies and Moths in Who Am I? Make a "pet" butterfly out of a clothespin.

BEACH DAYS

Be a Castle builder in the sand; put cardboard to use making easy Sand Molds and Sand Combs. Turn beach treasures into wearable art with Shell Jewelry. Learn how to "hear the ocean," create handy Trivets out of beach glass, and make a Candle in the sand. Keep the memories alive with an Ocean Diorama, and a Native American Sand Painting. Join a national Beach Clean-Up project; adopt a Sea Turtle or a Whale. Fish in your living room with Let's Go Fishin' and enjoy a healthy snack of Wiggly Fish!

AWAY AT CAMP

Ease kids' camp blues with yummy Brownies and "We Care" Packages! Keep track of the good times with a Camp Time-Line Scroll and a postcard banner.

LET'S MAKE AN IMPRESSION

Stamp up a storm with summer fruits and vegetables! Carve a potato into a Chinese Chop and make "Fingerprint" creatures. Looking for a great group project? Try a simple West African Adinkra cloth. Learn how to twist fabric into a fancy turban.

DOG-DAY AMUSEMENTS

The ultimate guide to beating those boring, there's-nothing-*fun*-to-do blues! Looking for an unusual hobby? Collect postmarks! Shoot marbles in a test of skill, build a city out of newspaper, scratch a picture, and make a frame out of candy! Looking for even more Summer fun? Learn to sew, preserve memories, set up a Home Restaurant, and play a Clothesline guessing game. Kids want to earn some money? Check out our Roadside Stand. No paint in the house? Whip up Paint-in-a-Pinch!

AN ICE CREAM PARTY

Throw a party! Stir up a Butterscotch Sauce and the Best Fudge Sauce for an unforgettable end to the season.

SUMMER WONDERS

Summer! Warm, glorious summer! School is out and kids are thrilled with the freedom. Three months of fun! Whether laid-back and easy or jam-packed with favorite pastimes, most kids will find themselves wanting to be out of doors this time of year.

- The days are long, hot, and sticky
- Short nights hang heavy and sparkle with fireflies
- Luscious, red strawberries ripen on the vine—ready for picking
- The air is filled with the hum of lawnmowers and the smell of freshly cut grass
- June 21 arrives, the summer solstice—marking the longest day of the year
- Hollyhock, larkspur, rose, nasturtium, and snapdragon perfume the air with their scent
- Bootes, "The Kite Constellation," is visible on a clear summer night
- Crickets chirp their welcome, as bees and other insects visit the garden
- The surf pounds the beach, as crabs play tag with the waves
- Ocean tidepools brim with life, and sea turtle hatchlings wander to the water's edge

A Night for Stargazing

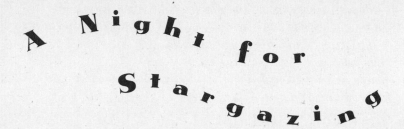

Imagine how many times the lines from this beloved poem, written in 1806, have been repeated by children! A clear summer night is a wonderful time for stargazing, and a great way to spend some time with the children in your life. It can be as simple as grabbing a blanket and lying on your backs together. With some kids few words need to be spoken—they're happy just to lie close and feast on the twinkling sights above them. Others will have a million questions! Either way, all kids will enjoy the stargazing activities that follow.

Stars are actually individual suns so many light-years away that they look like tiny specks of brightness. Light-years are a unit of distance astronomers use to determine the distance light travels in one year. (One light-year equals almost 6 trillion miles—that's nearly 10 trillion kilometers.) Light-years allow scientists to measure the distance between stars as well as the size of the various galaxies.

My Star Machine (AGES 5 AND UP, WITH HELP)

Children can make a tin-can planetarium and get to know the constellations. This is not only good practice, but great bedtime fun too! (This is an especially great activity for summer nights—kids stay up later, and adults are happy knowing the kids are entertained!) Babies and toddlers love to look at the stars on the ceiling too.

Astronomy books with star charts
Tracing paper
Pencil

TWINKLE, TWINKLE, LITTLE STAR

Twinkle, twinkle little star,
How I wonder what you are
Up above the world so high,
Like a diamond in the sky.

—JANE TAYLOR

STELLAR NEIGHBORS

The North Star—820 light-years from earth
Alpha Centauri—about 4 light-years from earth (this is the closest star that can be seen with the naked eye)

Scissors
Clear plastic glass about same diameter as containers (below)
Clean containers (we use the ones yogurt-covered raisins come in,
*   though any medium-size tin can works well)*
Hammer
1 large and 1 small nail
Blue construction paper
Black felt tip pen
Glue or tape
Flashlight (the Eveready Outdoor Area Light/Flashlight works best)
Facecloth
Heavy duty rubber bands
8 AA batteries (have a spare set on hand—kids may forget to turn
*   flashlights off)*

Simple Fun

Bedtime can be a trip through the Milky Way! Make dime-size dots on your child's ceiling with in-expensive Glo-in-the-dark fabric paint! When the lights go out, children can gaze up to find their very own twinkling sky! (Leave light on first for about 10 minutes to "activate"paint.)

Look through the astronomy books for some charts of various constellations. (We started with the Big Dipper.) Have the kids carefully trace the stars onto the tracing paper. Turn the plastic glass over the constellation and have them trace a circle around the stars. Cut out the circle, and place it (right side down) on the outside bottom of the container. Tape the paper in place. To make the stars, carefully tap the nails through each star on your drawing of the constellation—use the big nail for the larger stars and the small nail for the little stars of lesser magnitude. Cut the blue paper to fit the outside of the can, and tape or glue into place. Instruct kids to carefully print the name of the constellation on the blue paper. In a darkened room, place the flashlight inside the can (let the kids adjust the flashlight until the image is clear—try pulling the base of the flashlight down about $1/2$ inch if there is a bright spot) and cover the open end of the can and the flashlight with the facecloth and rubber band. Make up several cans, once children are familiar with a few of the better known groups of stars—the Big Dipper (which is visible year round), Orion, Draco, Cassiopeia, and Bootes—"The Kite" (easy to spot in the summer sky), they'll be anxious to move on to gazing at the real thing!

Note: *Kids in the Southern Hemisphere see a different group of stars. Their most popular constellation is called the Southern Cross.*

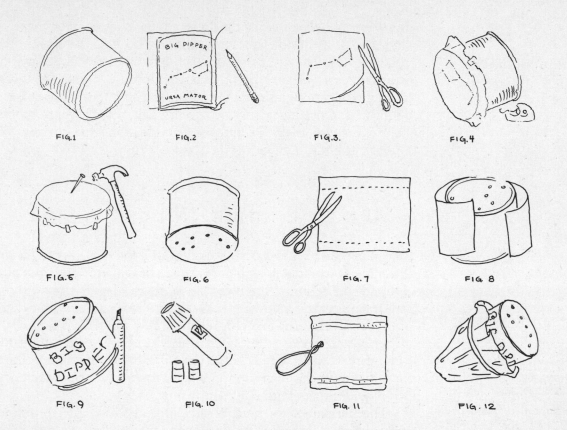

FIG.1 FIG.2 FIG.3. FIG.4

FIG.5 FIG.6 FIG.7 FIG 8

FIG.9 FIG.10 FIG.11 FIG.12

Tanabata

This Japanese celebration in honor of Vega and Altair takes place on July 7. The holiday features great displays of fireworks, sparklers, puppets, and paper decorations. Most lovely are the poems written by the children on long pieces of paper, which are then tied to the branches of trees. The fluttering ribbons are meant to represent the Milky Way.

The Legend of Tanabata

There once was a princess who was a weaver. Her name was Vega. She was in love with a shepherd whose name was Altair. Altair tended a herd of cows. One day when Vega was walking she met the young shepherd. The two young people fell in love, and could think of nothing but each other. Naturally, they forgot their tasks and were soon the target of the gods' wrath. With no milk, meat, or cloth, the gods decided the only thing to do was to separate the young lovers. They put one on each side of the Milky Way, far away from each other. Promptly, they reluctantly returned to work. It wasn't long though before the gods took pity on the star-crossed youngsters. Once a year, on the seventh day of the seventh month (July 7) the two lovers are allowed to walk across the heavens, on a bridge of birds, and be together.

UNDER THE NIGHT SKY

Stargazing can be intoxicating for all ages! If the kids in your life are like mine, it won't be long before they're begging for their first outdoor adventure under the night sky. This can be anything from a half-hour of giggling under blankets as the kids squeal with delight after identifying their first constellation, to a full-blown camp out! (Often younger kids are a bit terrified to be out of doors in the pitch-dark of night. If this is the case, I've found that letting them have their own flashlight not only gives them a sense of assurance, but provides them with entertainment as well.)

The best night for a starry adventure is a cloudless summer night when the moon is waxing—somewhere between a crescent and a first quarter moon. (Check the *Farmer's Almanac* for dates.)

Night Sky Essentials

- A planisphere—this is a moveable, circular map of the constellations, which shows the sky at various hours of the day and night. Align the time of day with the date—the window will show what the sky will look like at that moment. (See Kid-Source, this page.)
- Two or more flashlights—a high-powered one for adults to use as a "pointer," and regular-size ones for reading charts (plan on one per child).
- Red cellophane and an elastic—cover the end of the smaller flashlight and secure with the elastic (helps eyes stay adjusted to the dark).
- Binoculars.

KID-SOURCE

Kids can order a planisphere from The Nature Company, 800-227-1114.

- Insect repellent, beverages, and snacks.
- Sleeping bags, blankets, and pillows.

Note: *For an all-night camp out you'll need more food, utensils, paper plates and cups, foil, matches, trash bags, a resealable plastic bag, and a box of baby wipes for easy cleanup.*

Most people start by locating the Big Dipper, Polaris (the North Star), the Little Dipper, Orion, Bootes, and Vega—the brightest summer star. (Face north and look east. Vega is in the small constellation known as "Lyra," the harp.) Once the children have located Vega, they will enjoy hearing the Japanese fable associated with this star.

The Big Dipper, or How's Your Eye IQ?

(AGES 5 AND UP)

Ask most kids how many stars make up the Big Dipper, and most will answer "seven." Tell them to look carefully—the middle star of the handle (Mizar) has a teeny neighbor known as Alcor. Long before eye-testing charts were invented, the Mesopotamian and Arab people would use these stars to test people's vision. The Arabs called these neighboring stars the Horse and Rider, while Native Americans called them the Large Squaw with a Papoose on Her Back.

The Big Dipper, also known as Ursa Major, is probably the most widely recognized star pattern in the Northern Hemisphere. Most kids in this country think the constellation resembles a ladle. Children in other countries think it resembles something entirely different:

- Polynesian children call it the Rat
- Polish children call it the Wagon
- English children call it the Plough (Plow)
- Hindu children call it the Seven Wise Men

The Big Dipper is one of the easiest constellations to spot, as it is situated above the northern polar region, and is always visible as the earth turns. Face north to find the Big Dipper—it never sinks below the horizon, but circulates instead around the North Star, making a complete circle within a 24-hour period.

TWO FOR ONE

Did you know that Mizar is really a double star? (A double star is two stars orbiting around the same center of gravity, traveling through space together.) About 30 percent of the 200 billion stars in our galaxy are actually double stars!

Good Reading

- Anna Grossnickle Hines. *Sky All Around.* N.Y.: Clarion Books, 1989. (Ages 4 to 8)
- Clint Hatchett. *The Glow in the Dark Night Sky Book.* N.Y.: Random House, 1988. (Ages 7 and up)

The North Star

Before the invention of the compass, early man used the North Star for navigation. Constant, never appearing to move from its home directly over the North Pole, Polaris has guided countless people safely home. Columbus used the North Star to find the New World.

Locating the North Star   (AGES 5 AND UP)

Stand facing north. Locate the Big Dipper. Find Merak and Dubhe (known as the Pointers, they are the two brightest stars in the Big Dipper)—the two stars at the farthest end of the cup, away from the handle of the dipper. Trace an imaginary line in the sky, upward, about five times the distance between the two stars. There will be a lone, bright star—the North Star.

Note: *The North Star is also the tip of the handle in the Little Dipper.*

A Star Tracking Book   (AGES 5 AND UP)

Young astronomers will want to keep a record of their night findings. Kids can make simple books by folding several pieces of dark blue paper in half. Punch three holes along the folded edge and lace the pages together with string or yarn. Using any of the star guides, copy some constellations into the book. With a white pencil or crayon and a ruler draw each constellation onto a separate page. (Kids love this, as it's similar to dot-to-dot!) Instruct kids to leave enough room at the bottom of each page for the following information:

- Name of the constellation
- What the constellation is named for (animal, object, mythological character)
- When and where best observed
- A myth or short story associated with the star (may be entered on a separate piece of paper and kept inside the book)
- The child's pet name for the star grouping
- Personal observations

Midsummer's Eve

June 21, the day that marks the official beginning of summer! Also known as the summer solstice, or Midsummer's Eve, it is the longest day of the year—when the summer sun stays high in the sky and is the furthest north of the equator.

Though it is not observed widely in the United States, people throughout the world have been celebrating the summer solstice since ancient times. In past times the changes in the seasons were more closely observed—as crops and daily life were directly related to the changes in the natural world. Long ago in Europe, Midsummer's Eve was celebrated with great bonfires, as torch-lit processions were held throughout the land. Enormous wooden wheels were made to represent the sun. These were covered with layers of straw, set on fire, and rolled down the hillside. Some of the first fireworks are traced back to this festival. Twigs and vines were intertwined to form circular shapes, lit, and thrown high into the sky in praise of the sun and its life-giving force.

The Sun's Fade Out   (AGES 3 AND UP, WITH HELP)

What better day than the summer solstice to use the sun's energy in a fun art project. These pictures make great art to hang on the wall, or can be made into invitations for the next activity—a tea in honor of the wee woodland folk.

Light-sensitive paper (sold in school supply and toy stores)
Assorted objects—leaves, buttons, keys, large puzzle pieces, shells

Good Reading

Anne Hillerman. *Done in the Sun: Solar Projects for Children.* Santa Fe, NM: Sunstone Press, 1983. (Ages 6 to 10)

A TEA FOR THE FAIRYFOLK

There are fairies at the bottom of our garden!
They often have a dance on summer nights;
The butterflies and bees make a lovely little breeze,
And the rabbits stand about and hold the lights.
Did you know that they could sit upon the moonbeams
And pick a little star to make a fan,
And dance away up there in the middle of the air?
well, they can.

—ROSE FYLEMAN

Lay a sheet of the paper in the sun. Have children pick out objects they would like to see defined on the paper. Explain to children that the sun has a bleaching effect on the paper and wherever they place an object the paper will remain dark, as the object blocks the paper from the sun's rays. Arrange objects in a decorative manner. (Weight smaller objects with a small stone so they won't blow away in a breeze.) Leave the paper in direct sunlight for at least 4 hours—the longer the paper receives sunlight, the darker the paper under the object will appear.

A FAIRY'S TEA PARTY

Long considered a time of great merriment, magic, and whimsy, Midsummer's Eve is the perfect festival to introduce children to the imaginary world of fairies, elves, mossmen, and gnomes.

A tea party in honor of the tiny people who inhabit the woods is a celebration full of sheer delight and enchantment! Such make-believe play is a cornerstone of childhood and nurtures a child's imagination. We hold our party on the evening of June 24, the Feast of St. John the Baptist and the official Midsummer Day. Children will enjoy making the decorations, feasting on the Wacky Cake, and getting very silly while reading a Fairy's Tale. My mother often gave us warm milk or weak tea with honey in tiny little china cups, though children may also have fruit juice if they prefer.

Lovely Lanterns   (AGES 5 AND UP, WITH HELP)

These charming little paper lanterns create a magical atmosphere and are a must at any fairy tea party.

Fold a piece of 4- by 5-inch notepaper in half the long way. Line up a ruler along the folded edge and make a mark every $1/2$ inch along the entire length of the fold. Everywhere there is a mark, make a cut $1^1/2$ inches long. (Be careful not to cut all the way to the end. There should be a $1/2$-inch border along the open side.) Open up the piece of paper and tape the short sides together. To help the lantern hold its shape, press both ends in to the middle and recrease the middle fold. String several together with needle and thread to create a garland.

Note: *If the children have planted Chinese lanterns in their garden this is the night to put them to use. The bright orange globes look wonderful in a garland by themselves, or try alternating them with the paper lanterns. The sight of them dancing in the night air is sure to entice any fairies that may be watching!*

The Tablesetting

Some of you might be wondering what fairies use for their tablecloths. Well, from what I have heard they traipse through the woods in the wee hours of the morning in search of *spiderwebs!* Sparkling as they do with the morning mist, it's a temptation too hard for a fairy to resist!

Fairy tea parties are the perfect occasion to bring out any lace tablecloths you might have. Either cloth or paper will do. Use any doll or play dishes that the children have—fairies are tiny folk, and grown-up dishes just won't do! Nut cups, tiny baskets, miniature plastic cups, and tiny umbrellas work perfectly too. Check with your local party supply store.

A Fairy's Tale   (ALL AGES)

This little story is a silly pastime we use to entertain the children after they have enjoyed their refreshments. You can use the one we have written, or let children make up their own version. One person is the storyteller. (An adult or an older child who reads well.) Younger children can take turns "filling in the blanks" whenever the reader comes to a blank space in the story (_____) by picking a card out of the envelope. If you have some artists in your group enlist their help in drawing a picture of the item mentioned on each card. That way, young kids who can't read yet can join in by naming the picture on the card that they pick. Alternatively, cut pictures that represent the items out of magazines and catalogues.

Using index cards or slips of paper, write out a list of 24 phrases—ask kids to think of about 12 things from nature and about 12 common or gross and yucky things (this is their favorite part, though adults will want to set limits!), or use our suggestions. Draw or glue a picture of the thing named onto each card if desired. Place all of the cards in a large envelope or bowl.

Simple Fun

Make Fairy Paint—children's artwork will "sparkle"! Mix 1 cup Epsom salt with 1 cup water. Boil till dissolved, then cool. Provide kids with construction paper (in dark blue or purple) and some crayons (in pastel colors). Have children draw a picture. Dip a brush in the Fairy Paint and brush over the entire picture. As the picture dries, lovely crystals will form!

Simple Fun

Make a fairy wand. Trace two 5-inch stars onto pastel-colored paper or felt. Glue the stars together, inserting a chopstick or stick in between them for a handle. Decorate with "fairy dust" (silver and gold glitter) and colorful ribbon streamers.

Butterfly wings	Dirty socks
Bumblebees	An old tin can
Spiderwebs	Thumbtacks
Toadstools	Coat hangers
Rose petals	A flat tire
A rainbow	Dog food
A lizard	Wet leaves
Bird feathers	Three dragons
Five acorns	A snake
Kitten whiskers	Moldy bread
Rotten apples	Melted ice cream
Sawdust	Soggy towels
Two slimy frogs	Rusty nails

Read the following story out loud. Whenever you come to a blank space (_____) have a child draw a card and say the word or phrase to everyone.

Once upon a time, deep in the woods of a far-off land, there lived the Queen of the Fairies and her merry band. It was the middle of June, quite near to the most special night of all, Midsummer's Eve, when the fairy folk held their moonlight ball! Each of the fairy folk went off into the woods, thinking hard, as to what special item they would bring to the ball to please the Queen.

The first fairy went into her house and reached under the bed for the _____ she had been saving all year. "I know this will please the Queen," she said. Her neighbor, the Old Troll, said, "I have an idea! I will bake a cake. I will put _____ in the batter, and _____ on top of the frosting!" "Yes, yes," said Tabitha, the littlest fairy of them all, "I will bring _____ and _____ for all to enjoy!" "We'll need to get _____ and _____ too." said Tinker. "Everyone had them last year." "Splendid!" said Belinda, the oldest and wisest of them all. "I shall make a tablecloth for the party. I'll sew _____ and _____ all around the edges! And I'll make fancy napkins, with _____ and _____ on them!"

So the fairies busied themselves throughout the day, as they gathered all the items that they would bring to the party on Midsummer's Eve. As evening came they were putting the last touches on the celebration. There were great big bowls full of _____ and _____, and platters of _____ and _____. Great bouquets of flowers with _____ stood on each little table. At each place setting was a gift of _____ from the Queen Fairy. Some of the fairies brought _____ and _____, while the trolls brought _____, _____, and _____. Long after nightfall, and up until the first rays of the sun, the woods rang with their laughter and merriment. Certainly it had been the best night of the year, and they couldn't wait until the following summer, for the next Midsummer's Eve celebration. That party would be even better—with _____ and _____ for dessert!

Geralyn's Wacky Cake

Considering the crazy party the fairies have, this cake is appropriately named! Children will find it very simple to make, as the batter can all be mixed together in one big bowl. A must for all little first-time bakers.

> 3 cups flour
> 6 tablespoons dry cocoa
> 1/2 teaspoon salt
> 2 teaspoons baking soda
> 2 cups sugar
> 2 tablespoons vinegar
> 2 teaspoons vanilla
> 3/4 cup oil
> 2 cups water

Preheat oven to 350°F. Add all ingredients together in one large bowl and blend well. Grease and flour a 9- by 13-inch pan. Pour the batter into the pan and bake for about 30 minutes. Cool on a rack before frosting.

Note: *The batter may also be used for cupcakes: use paper liners and fill each cup half way. Bake for about 15 minutes. Yields about 24 cupcakes.*

WOODLAND LORE

• Fairies and other woodland folk only come out at night, when no one can see them. During the day they masquerade as birds, butterflies, and bees!

• If you come across a circle of mushrooms in a clearing, it is known as a Fairy Ring, and is sure to bring you good luck!

• If you come across the plant known as the Dutchman's Breeches, be sure to leave them! They are really the white britches belonging to the elves, who've left them in the sun to dry!

Good Reading

• Rose Fyleman. *A Fairy Went a Marketing*. N.Y.: Dutton Children's Books, 1990. (Ages 3 to 7)
• Cicely Mary Barker. *Flower Fairies Activity Book*. N.Y.: Frederick Warne, 1992. (All ages)

Buttercream Frosting

4 tablespoons butter
2¹/₂ cups confectioners' sugar
¹/₄ teaspoon salt
1 teaspoon vanilla
1 tablespoon cream

In the bowl of a mixer, cream the butter until light and fluffy. Add 1 cup of the sugar, the salt, and the vanilla. Blend well. Add the remaining sugar, along with the cream, and blend well.

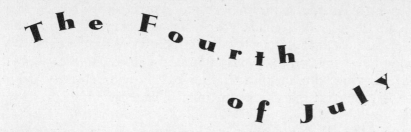

The Fourth of July

With its parades, flags, and fireworks the Fourth of July is a highlight of summer and a celebration children look forward to. Also known as Independence Day, the Fourth of July honors the adoption of the Declaration of Independence, on July 4, 1776.

A Quill Pen (AGES 4 AND UP)

In the spirit of the holiday, children can sign their own important documents with a quill pen—just like people did back in the 1700s. Summer is the perfect season to visit local petting zoos and game preserves and perhaps find a feather to use. Fallen feathers from turkey or geese are perfect, but be sure to ask permission first. (If there aren't any zoos or farms in your area, check the yellow pages for local craft stores that stock feathers.)

Using scissors or a sharp knife (adults only), cut the end of the quill at an angle, to form a sharp point. Cut a small slit in the middle of the point to catch the ink. Dip the end of the pen in the ink (try Blueberry Ink, below), and write. Children can practice on scrap paper first, until they get the hang of it. Wash and dry the point carefully after every use, and trim the end every so often as it wears down with use.

Blueberry Ink

Blueberries are plentiful in summer and make a wonderful ink.

¹/₂ cup blueberries
¹/₂ teaspoon salt
¹/₂ teaspoon lemon juice
Water, for thinning

Place the blueberries in the bowl of a food processor or blender and process for about 30 seconds. With a spatula, scrape the berries and all of the juice into a strainer set over a bowl. With the back of a spoon, press the berries to extract all of the juice. Stir the salt and the lemon juice into the blueberry juice. Thin with a bit of water if the ink seems too thick. Store the ink in a clean jar.

Note: *Be sure to save and freeze the blueberry pulp to add to your Bird-seed treats!*

A Holiday Drum

(AGES 4 AND UP)

What Fourth of July celebration would be complete without a drum! Younger children especially love to bang on a drum and hold an impromptu parade. Let children decide what color their drum will be and how they want to decorate it—white with red and blue stars, red with blue stars, blue with red stars.

An empty cylinder-shaped oatmeal box
Red, white, and blue construction paper
Blue or red paint
Brush (optional)
Yarn (red or blue)
Fabric (red or blue)
Scissors
A hole puncher
Glue
Fourth of July stickers, stars, glitter, etc. (optional)

Simple Fun

Try Red, White, and Blue-berries! Top vanilla ice cream with strawberries and blueberries—red, white, and blueberries for the Fourth of July!

Remove the lid from the box and set aside. Paint the oatmeal box or cover it with a sheet of construction paper. Trim the paper as necessary and glue it in place. Poke a hole on opposite sides of the box and run a long piece of yarn through it. Tie the ends together. Place the lid on the fabric and cut out two circles that are 2 inches larger in diameter than the lid. Punch holes around the edges of the circles with the hole puncher, or scissors, spacing them about every 2 inches. Replace the lid on the top of the box. Place one fabric circle on top of the box and secure with a few drops of glue. Glue the remaining fabric circle to the other end of the box. Cut a very long piece of yarn and knot one end. Thread the yarn through one of the holes in the fabric, and lace the yarn back and forth through the top and the bottom holes all around the box. Knot the end. Decorate the sides of the drum as desired with stars, glitter, or stickers. Little children are safest using metal spoons for drumsticks, though older kids may enjoy making their own: Make a slight slit in a small rubber ball and push a pencil or $1/4$-inch dowel inside.

Good Reading

James C. Gilbin. *Fireworks, Picnics & Flags: The Story of the Fourth of July Symbols.* N.Y.: Clarion Books, 1983. (Ages 7 to 11)

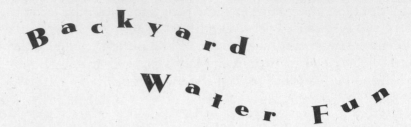

Backyard Water Fun

Simple Fun

Have a Watermelon Seed Spitting Contest! Draw a circle on a large white piece of paper on the ground. Try shooting the seed into the circle! Or see who can spit the farthest—draw a chalk-line on the ground and mark off in one-foot increments. Good luck!

Not all kids are fortunate enough to have a place to swim during the long, hot days of summer. For our refreshing summertime fun, all kids need are a hose, a few common household supplies, a grassy area, and a bit of imagination! Children can beat the heat with their friends with these fun projects.

The Water Snake   (Ages 5 and Up, with Help)

Kids can make their garden hose come "alive" with this simple project. Drive a wooden stake, a heavy wooden dowel, or old mop handle about a foot or so into the ground. (A few whacks with a hammer will help secure it.) Tie a hose to the stake, leaving the first two feet of hose free, to act as the "snake." Turn on the water and watch the hose come alive as the water pressure makes the hose whip and toss. You may need to adjust the water pressure and the length of the hose that hangs free, to get the right effect.

Simple Fun

Toddlers enjoy spraying each other with plastic spray bottles. Run containers through a hot dishwasher to clean thoroughly, then fill with clean, cold water for spraying.

The Ultimate Slide   (All Ages, with Supervision)

Kids will need a 20-foot length of heavy plastic (available at a hardware store) and some gallon jugs filled with water to set up this fun project. Look for a sloping, grassy area with enough room to get a running start. Lay the plastic down and secure the ends with the water jugs. Set up a sprinkler, and place off to the side, but close enough to keep the plastic soaked with water. Have the kids take turns sliding down the plastic and through the sprinkler.

Note: *Try to move the plastic about every half hour to avoid any damage to the grass.*

Water Balloons

(ALL AGES)

Some old-fashioned fun with water balloons is a good end to a hot summer day. Keep a big bag of colorful balloons on hand for the kids to fill up. When they tire of lobbing them at each other, suggest playing catch with some old rubber gloves filled with water. Tie the wrists securely with string or rubber bands and have the kids try a game of Hot Potato!

Icy Cold Treats

After all the hard play, kids will want to relax and enjoy some of our refreshing treats.

• Fill ice cube trays with fruit juice. When frozen solid, float the cubes in carbonated water or ginger ale. Children especially love some of the novelty ice cube trays in fun shapes—porpoises, stars, cowboy boots, or fruit shapes.

• Cut chilled, ½-inch slices of watermelon into decorative shapes with cookie cutters. Make "Melon Slush" from leftovers: Place melon in blender. Add a spoonful of honey, a couple of ice cubes, and a big scoop of yogurt. Puree till smooth and serve in a big glass!

Good Reading

• John Cassidy. *The Unbelievable Bubble Book.* Palo Alto, CA: Klutz Press, 1987. (All ages)
• Nancy White Carlstrom. *Better Not Get Wet, Jesse Bear.* N.Y.: Macmillan, 1988. (Ages 3 to 6)

Simple Fun (or How to Get Inside a Giant Bubble!)

Fill a garbage can lid with bubble mixture—1 cup dishwashing liquid and 10 cups water. Make a circle out of wire (attach two opened coat hangers together) and wrap it with yarn. Place the wire circle in the soap. Have a child stand inside the circle with her arms at her side. Quickly pull the hoop up over her head! Kids can also place waterproof toys in the soap to enclose them in a bubble too.

Fireflies

Fireflies! Who can remember a summer without these magical little creatures? Also known as the lightning bug, the firefly is actually a type of winged beetle. There are many species of fireflies, each with its own flash pattern. They are most active July through September, and children will find them especially visible from right after dusk until midnight.

The average person doesn't realize that the bursts of light that these curious bugs emit are actually part of an elaborate mating ritual. Fireflies can't hear or smell, so the males alight and signal to the short-winged females on the ground. There the female lays her glowing eggs in a bed of loose soil. The larvae, known as glowworms, snuggle into their nest, where they will grow for the next two years. Kids will be interested to know that each tiny larva has a light on its abdomen and that fireflies glow their whole lives!

A Firefly Lamp   (AGES 5 AND UP)

Summer is the season most adults allow children to stay up a bit later than usual. Pick a night when the dark is aglow with the tiny sparks of fireflies—and the children will be richly rewarded! Such a night is perfect to make a firefly lamp.

Find a clean, wide-mouthed plastic jar. Tap several holes in the top of the lid with a nail. Tap two holes near the top of the jar, one on each side, and lace a length of twine through for a handle. (Make sure the knots are on the inside of the jar so the twine doesn't interfere with the lid.) Instruct kids to catch as many fireflies as they can—this is not an easy task, so adults may want to join in the fun! Catch fireflies by cupping your hands or by using a fine-mesh bug net. Carefully place the fireflies in the jar. Continue catching fireflies until the "lamp" emits enough light to glow softly.

FIREFLY

. . . I never could have thought
*   of it,*
To have a little bug all lit
And made to go on wings.

—ELIZABETH MADOX
  ROBERTS

City Watch

Look for fireflies around grass and bushes and in parks!

Simple Fun

Give kids flashlights and let them pretend they are "fireflies" by signaling to each other.

Children love to sit around the lamp and tell stories. Do be sure and let the fireflies free after a while, as they will be anxious to get on with their business.

The Warm Water Trick

(AGES 5 AND UP, WITH SUPERVISION)

Before the children set all of their winged friends free, you can show them how temperature affects the flashes the fireflies make. The warmer the temperature (the hotter the summer night), the less time between flashes. Fill a bowl full of warm water, about 80 to 83°F., and partially submerge the lamp into the water, being careful not to let the water seep into the jar. Note how the fireflies increase their flashes. Warn children not to exceed the suggested temperature or to keep them in the warm water too long—the fireflies will become lethargic and they might cause them harm.

Hey, Mr. Firefly!

(AGES 5 AND UP)

Once children have let the fireflies free from the jar, it's time to let them join in on the courting game. Have kids grab a penlight flashlight and sit on the ground near a large concentration of airborne

AMERICAN FIREFLY FOLKLORE

• In parts of the South it is considered good luck if a firefly flies in your house!
• On a given night, if the fireflies are flying high it's likely to rain the next day.

Good Reading

• *Ranger Rick Magazine*. National Wildlife Federation, 1412 Sixteenth Street, N.W., Washington, D.C. 20036. 1-800-432-6564. $14.00 for a one-year subscription (great for ages 6-12).
• Julie Brinckloe. *Fireflies*. N.Y.: Macmillan, 1985. (Ages 4 to 8)

males. Instruct them to fix their eyes on one flash and see if they can coax him in: Wait two seconds after his flash (count 1001, 1002 . . .), hold the flashlight down near the grass, and flash for about 1 second. Repeat this sequence, and see if the firefly will come close.

Note: *Older kids are often able to note a pattern to the flashes of individual fireflies. Have them look for differences in the time between flashes, as well as the color and intensity of the light. Point out that certain species of fireflies come out right after dusk, while others wait until almost midnight to appear. Some are highfliers, while others stay low to the ground. And don't forget to watch for a female down in the grass—she will keep answering her mate's flashes until he joins her.*

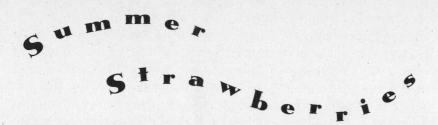

Red, juicy, and ripe with the essence of summer, strawberries herald the arrival of warm weather. In fact, strawberries' flavor improves as the temperature rises! The best-tasting berries of course are the ones you pick yourself—look for bright red berries that are fully ripe for the sweetest flavor. Patches of green or yellow signal an underripe and tasteless berry.

Strawberry picking is an activity that kids love—though they usually end up putting more in their mouths than in the basket! If you don't grow your own, then be sure to visit one of the pick-your-own farms in your area. (Check the local newspaper, or try the yellow pages for your county's cooperative extension service for more information.)

The best time to pick berries is on a slightly overcast morning. Kids will be more comfortable and strawberries are easier to spot when not in the full glare of a bright sun. Once kids have a basket full of berries, there are endless ways to enjoy them: Try them sliced over vanilla yogurt, sliced and served with cream and a bit of brown sugar, or dipped in chocolate. For some old-fashioned fun, try cooking them outdoors!

Sunshine Strawberry Preserves

Most kids know about Sun Tea, but have they ever heard of cooking strawberries in the sun? This is an old-time recipe that needs to be started in the morning on a clear, sunny day.

1 quart strawberries, rinsed and hulled
1 cup sugar
1 teaspoon lemon juice

Place the strawberries, sugar, and lemon juice in a heavy saucepan and bring to a boil. Cook over medium heat for about 7 minutes, stirring occasionally. Pour the mixture into a shallow pan and allow to cool. When it is room temperature, cover the pan with a layer of plastic wrap, and place outside in direct sunlight. (Place on a table or chair so that curious animals won't disturb it.) Allow the preserves to sit outside for the whole day, checking on it periodically. Bring the container indoors before dusk and refrigerate overnight. The following morning, remove the plastic wrap and stir the berries gently with a spoon. Reposition the cover and place the pan outside to allow berries to soak up the sun as before. Repeat the procedure for one more day to produce a nice, thick preserve. Pour the preserves into sterile jars, and store in the refrigerator. Use as you would any strawberry jam.

Variation: Try making Strawberries 'n' Butter: Mix equal amounts of Sunshine Strawberry Preserves and softened, unsalted butter. Yummy over toast, bagels, waffles, and pancakes.

Good Reading

Jennifer Coldrey. *Strawberry*. Morristown, N.J.: Silver Burdett Press, 1989. (Ages 3 to 10)

Strawberry Shortcake

I couldn't resist adding this recipe—it's been my own, absolute, number-one favorite dessert since childhood! As far as I am concerned, only two rules apply: The shortcakes must be homemade, warm, and slathered with butter, and the berries must be topped with freshly whipped cream. Let the kids pick out the best berries to decorate the top!

For the strawberries

> *1¹/₂ quarts strawberries, washed and hulled (reserve a few choice ones for the top)*
> *¹/₂ cup sugar*

Mash the berries slightly with a fork and combine with the sugar. Set aside until needed. (Kids love helping with this part. We often put the berries in a huge bowl and use a potato masher.)

For the shortcake

2 cups flour
4 teaspoons baking powder
1/4 teaspoon salt
2 1/2 tablespoons sugar
1/3 cup unsalted butter, cut into bits
2/3 cup light cream

Preheat the oven to 350°F. and place a rack in the center of the oven. Sift the dry ingredients together in a large bowl. Cut in the butter with a pastry cutter, or two forks or knives. Gradually add the cream and mix lightly. Flour a work surface, and turn the mixture onto it. Shape mixture into one large shortcake and pat down in a buttered round cake pan. Cook in the oven for about 20 minutes or until the top has turned a pale golden brown. Cool the shortcake slightly, then split into two layers with a bread knife. Butter each layer on the cut side. Place the bottom half, buttered side up, on a large platter. Top with half of the prepared strawberries. Place the other half of the shortcake on top, buttered side down, and pour the remaining berries over the top. Add whipped cream in a big dollop, and let the kids decorate with their choice strawberries.

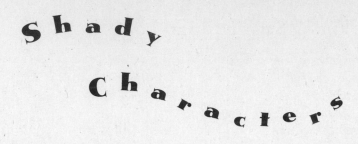

Little heads need to be protected from the hot summer sun—try these simple toppers to keep kids cool and in the shade! (Paper hats make great summer birthday activities or favors too.)

An Easy Newspaper Topper (AGES 5 AND UP)

Fold a double sheet of newspaper in half, the short way. Fold the two upper corners down, into the middle, so that they meet. Fold the bottom edge of one side of the hat, so that it meets the two corners. Fold it again to make a sturdy cuff. Repeat with the bottom edge of the other side. Open up the hat and place on the child's head. Hats may be left plain or painted and decorated with feathers, jewels, and stickers. (Secure the ends of the hat with colorful paper clips for added strength.) Here are some easy variations on our Newspaper Topper.

Sou'wester:

Roll up the bottom edge of the hat instead of folding. Punch two holes in the front and tie on strings in case of strong winds!

Middle Eastern Turban:

Follow directions for Newspaper Topper, but begin with a double sheet folded down an inch or two along the top edge. With the fold away from you, and on the other side, continue as above. Fold the corners into the middle of the hat and tuck under the center flaps.

The Ultimate Summer Brim

(AGES 5 AND UP,
WITH HELP)

This hat has a cute rolled brim that kids can wear in the front or the back, as the mood suits them! Add a few paper flowers (page 89) for a fancy touch. Hats may be left plain or painted—try stripes or polka dots for a whimsical look.

Cut five triangles out of a double thickness of newspaper. (Other similar-weight paper may be used instead of newspaper, but make sure it's pliable enough to fold up the brim.) Triangles should measure 10 inches at the base, 10 inches on the side, and 2 inches wide near the top. You will have ten triangles. Glue two triangles together, for a total of five triangles. Paint if desired, and allow to dry. Using a hole puncher, punch holes the length of both sides of each triangle. Using colorful yarn, have the kids lace the five triangles together. (Put two triangles together, wrong sides facing each other, and stitch up one edge. Repeat, until all of the triangles are attached to each other. Stitch the two remaining sides together to form the hat.) Place on a child's head, and roll up brim.

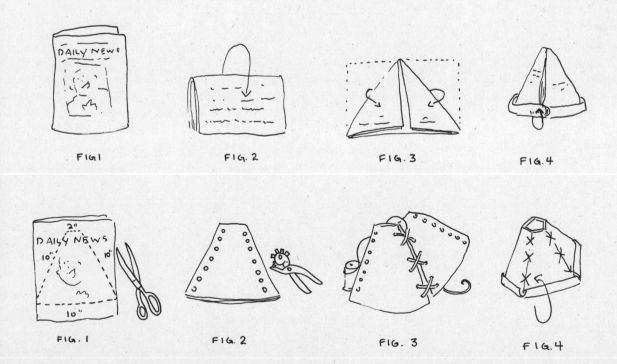

FIG. 1   FIG. 2   FIG. 3   FIG. 4

FIG. 1   FIG. 2   FIG. 3   FIG. 4

More Lids for the Kids (Ages 5 and Up)

Grab some paper plates and provide kids with an array of decorative items—feathers, jewels, lace, paper doilies, sequins, and assorted ribbons to use for tying. Let the kids decorate the plates. Punch a hole on each side of the plate and tie under chin with ribbon. Add fruit for a Carmen Miranda–style hat!

The Little "Summer" Gardener

Once the spring garden has matured, children will be anxious to harvest their crops. Encourage them to munch a few veggies fresh from the garden, once they've been rinsed off to get rid of any grit.

Children will jump at this suggestion—any chance to play with water is well received! Unless kids have grown the monster varieties, for the best taste try to have them pick the vegetables before they grow too big. Be sure to harvest all the vegetables. Kids can pile extras in a big basket and share them with friends and neighbors.

One of the greatest benefits of a child's garden is that kids are much more likely to eat something that they have grown themselves, especially if they are allowed to lend a hand in the kitchen. My son's favorite way to eat his vegetables is with a light cheese sauce on top.

Hunter's Cheese Sauce

I make a double recipe of this once a month and freeze individual portions in an ice cube tray. Keep cubes in a large resealable plastic bag and melt one or two as needed.

2 cups milk, warmed
3 tablespoons butter
3 tablespoons unbleached white flour
1 cup grated cheddar cheese
1/2 teaspoon dry mustard

Good Reading

Lois Ehlert. *Growing Vegetable Soup*. N.Y.: Harcourt Brace Jovanovich, 1990. (Ages 3 to 6)

I eat my peas with honey,
I've done it all my life.
It makes the peas taste funny,
but it keeps them on my knife.

— UNKNOWN

City Watch

Warm the milk in a saucepan over low heat. Turn the heat to the lowest setting and set aside until needed. Melt the butter in a saucepan over low heat. Turn the heat to medium, add the flour and whisk for a few minutes. Gradually add the warm milk, whisking all the while. Cook, stirring, until smooth and thick. Add the cheese and blend until it's melted and the sauce is smooth. Stir in the dry mustard, and set aside to cool slightly. Serve at once or freeze for later use.

Note: *You may use 2 tablespoons white flour and 1 tablespoon whole wheat flour for added nutrition.*

That's My Name! (AGES 3 AND UP)

Considering the fact that children spend most of their time out of doors in the summer, here are some fun gardening projects to try. Kids will get a kick out of seeing their names spelled out in plants. Kids can write their names or initials in mustard, cress, or lettuce (try one of the heat-tolerant lettuces such as Little Gem or Red Salad Bowl). All kids need is a few feet of space, seed packets, and a fat stick about 5 inches long. Have the kids scratch out their names or initials in the soil. Press the stick into the soil, following the outline of the letters, to make a furrow for the seeds. Sow seeds and tamp down the soil firmly. Water gently so as not to disturb the seeds. Have kids check the seeds daily and water as necessary to keep the soil moist.

The Great Pumpkin Contest

(AGES 3 AND UP, WITH HELP)

Summer is the perfect season for planning a contest to see who can grow the biggest pumpkin! As most pumpkins take about 115 days to mature, have kids plant their seeds in time for the pumpkin harvest to coincide with Halloween or some other autumn festival. Plant seeds following the directions on the seed packet. (Pumpkins are usually grown in a hill, with two or three plants per hill. Hills need to be about 8 feet apart from each other.) Each child is in charge of caring for his own pumpkin. Be sure that all kids entering the contest get to win by setting up various categories—the biggest, the roundest, the deepest "pumpkin" color, most unusual shape, and so forth.

Here's a tip to get a jump on the competition: Once the pumpkins have reached the size of an orange, pick off most of the pumpkins on the vine so that there are only two or three left growing. Once the remaining pumpkins have grown to the size of soccer balls, choose the ones kids want to be their entries, and remove the rest of the pumpkins.

After kids have chosen their entry, they can carve their name in the skin and watch it "grow"! Provide kids with a nail and let them scratch their first name in the skin of the pumpkin—don't let them dig too deeply; they should just scrape off the outer layer of skin.

Note: *Pumpkins thrive on rich soil and lots of water. My children and I once started our seeds in our compost pile, with great results!*

Best Pumpkin Varieties

- Largest—Atlantic Giant, Big Max, The Great Pumpkin
- Best Shape—Spooktacular, Baby Bear, Tom Fox, Connecticut Field
- Most "Pumpkin" Color—Rouge D'Etampes, Landreth Cheese
- Most Unusual Color—Lumina Cream Colored, White Cheese Pumpkin

Good Reading

Steven Kroll. *The Biggest Pumpkin Ever.* N.Y.: Scholastic Books, 1985. (Ages 3 to 6)

Calling All Butterflies!

Little gardeners from the country or the city can attract butterflies to their garden, as all these flowers can be planted in containers. Plant seeds according to the directions on the seed packet and set containers in a sunny spot. Children should check the plants daily and keep the soil most. Once flowers are in bloom kids can keep a look out for the butterflies to arrive. And what excitement there will be on that day! The Papago Indians of North America believed that butterflies were made from sunlight and the fragments of colored flowers sent to earth to "make the hearts of children dance."

RAINBOW WINGS

Rural Americans often predicted the summer weather according to the color of the butterfly's wings: white meant rain; dark meant thunder; and yellow meant sunshine.

Favorite Blooms

- Indian Paintbrush—brilliant rays of red and yellow.
- Butterfly weed—reddish orange. Along with magenta, this is a color favored by butterflies.
- Daylily—the orange varieties; especially loved by the Swallowtail butterfly.
- Purple Coneflower—a pink to dark rose sun lover.
- Hyssop—both Monarch and Swallowtail butterflies are attracted by the bright blue flowers.

Also consider: honeysuckle, cosmos, aster, daisy, verbena, thyme, lavender, lantana, or pineapple sage.

Note: *Male butterflies love to gather in water. Kids can provide a place for them to meet by setting out a shallow dish of water.*

There are over 28,000 species of butterflies. More than 700 types live in the United States alone, with 200 types living in

Florida. Butterflies have a life expectancy of about ten to fourteen days, though some species living in the tropics can live for up to eighteen months. Nectar and pollen of flowers are the feast of choice, though fermented fruit is a favorite too. Butterflies perch while feeding and so are especially fond of flowers with a broad head. These lovely winged insects are most active on a warm summer day, as they can't fly when their body temperature drops below 86°F.—making summer the prime season for children to observe them.

The Giant Swallowtail is the largest butterfly in the United States, with a wingspan of from 4 to 6 inches. The Common Sulphur is the most prolific in the eastern part of the state—legend has it that this species, with its buttery yellow color, is the reason the insect came to be known as the "butterfly." The smallest butterfly in the United States is the Pygmy Blue, which makes its home in the southeastern states. The Monarch Butterfly is considered the greatest traveler; known by its striking black and orange color, this species can fly over 2,000 miles during its annual migration.

Good Reading

Mathew Tekulsky. *The Butterfly Garden: Turning Your Window Box or Backyard into a Beautiful Home for Butterflies.* Boston: Harvard Common Press, 1989. (Ages 8 to adult)

Who Am I?   (Ages 3 and Up)

Many children have a hard time telling the difference between a butterfly and a moth. A fun nature project is getting up close and observing the differences between the two. Here's what to have kids look out for.

Butterfly	Moth
Antennae with thin knobs at the ends	Antennae with pointed or feathered ends
Slender body	Fat and furry body
Rests with wings closed	Rests with wings open
Active mostly during day	Nocturnal, active at night

Nocturnal Note

The night-visiting Hummingbird Sphinx Moth will charm children on a summer night. Quite similar to a hummingbird, this little creature hovers while feeding. Plant some sweetly fragrant nicotiana, and let kids watch for any visitors!

Clothespin Butterflies (AGES 3 AND UP, WITH HELP)

While children wait for their plants to blossom they can make their own butterflies! (Wooden clothespins make all the difference with this simple, homemade toy.) Stack several layers of differently colored tissue paper, and cut into 6-inch squares. Pinch the stack together in the middle to form "wings" and gently slide the clothespin down the center. Make antennas by folding a pipe cleaner in half and gluing it on top. Glue tiny wooden or plastic beads on each end. Glue on two plastic "wiggly"eyes or draw eyes on with a felt tip marker.

Beach Days

It's summer, it's hot, and the kids are full of restless energy. Whether you're lucky enough to live near the water's edge, or are several hours away, what better way to spend a lazy summer day than at the beach!

Castles in the Sand (ALL AGES)

Having grown up in Florida, I have seen my share of sand castles. My favorite type are the lovely, somewhat delicate looking drip-castles my mother was so fond of and dearly loved to build for me when I was a child. Here is her method: First, build a big mound of damp sand. Find a piece of flat driftwood and carve the mound into a uniform shape: rectangle, pyramid, or square. Next, scoop up a handful of sopping wet sand, tilt your hand slightly, and let the watery sand run down the side of your fingers. By doing this, here and there, my mother would create the most magical spires and turrets. All of a sudden our sand castle would come to life, and for the next few hours we would imagine princesses, princes, and dragons. Anyone can build a similar castle—all it takes is imagination. Gather bits of seaweed and small sticks for bushes. Place a seagull feather or two for a flag. Build a moat around the castle and float small objects for boats. Make a drawbridge from a small, flat piece of driftwood. Make windows and doors by pressing small shells or stones into the sand.

Sand Combs (AGES 5 AND UP)

We always make these easy combs before we head off for a day at the beach. The children can amuse themselves for quite a while as they swirl the combs through the sand. Take a heavy piece of card-

Good Reading

Dennis Nolan. *The Castle Builder.* N.Y.: Aladdin Books, 1993. (Ages 4 and up)

AT THE SEASIDE

When I was down beside the sea
a wooden spade they gave to me
to dig the sandy shore.
My holes were empty like a cup,
in every hole the sea came up,
Til it could come no more.

—ROBERT LOUIS STEVENSON

Simple Fun

Cut the top off a large cardboard juice container for a simple sand mold. Pack wet sand inside. Great for sand castles!

board and cut it into a strip about 12 to 14 inches long and about 3 to 4 inches wide. Make "teeth" along one of the sides by cutting out 1- by 1-inch notches. Kids can swirl circles and various other designs by gently "combing" the cardboard through the sand. It helps to clear off an area on the beach before starting, being careful to remove any large shells, stones, or other debris that might spoil the design.

Shell Jewelry

(AGES 5 AND UP)

Making necklaces, bracelets, and ankle-bracelets out of shells is a great quiet-time activity. Many shells found on the beach will already have holes in them. If not, try tapping a small, sharp nail into the shell with a hammer. (Some kids enjoy working with a simple, nonelectric hand drill. Try a 1.5 drill bit for making holes. Just be sure to put a small piece of masking tape on the shell first to keep the drill bit from slipping.) Shell jewelry is fun to wear throughout the year—it's a great reminder of summer!

Thin, colorful pieces of ribbon, or dental floss or string
Thin elastic (for bracelets and ankle bracelets)
Scissors
Assorted shells

Thread the shells onto the ribbon. Some children like to tie each shell in place, while others like to string on a few and let them dangle in a bunch. Tie the ends together in a knot.

Note: *Children can also paint the shells with poster paint or acrylic for a different effect. Once the paint is dry, apply a coat of acrylic, water base sealer for protection.*

More Fun with Shells (ALL AGES)

Children love to gather shells at the beach. Provide kids with cups, buckets, and scoops to explore the sand and see what treasures the tide has washed up. Encourage your beach-goers to fill their buckets with shells of all sizes—there are lots of fun uses for the shells once they get home.

- Large scallop shells make great spoon rests for the kitchen.
- Abalone shells (or any large shell) can be used to hold soaps in the bathroom (sea creature soaps are especially nice).
- Shells make great catch-alls for kids' rooms—fill with barrettes, jacks, gum, or small treasures.
- Create crazy creatures: Try gluing shells together to make funny animals or people.
- Try pasting tiny shells on note cards to use as greeting cards.
- Start a shell collection by piling them in clear jars (check the library for a book on shells—learn the shells' names and all about who lived in them).
- Make a "Beachscape"—arrange shells on a shelf with interesting pieces of driftwood, skate cases, starfish, and other ocean treasures.
- Glue shells onto an inexpensive barrette, frame, or box.
- Make a windchime: Tie individual shells on lengths of string attached to a piece of driftwood.
- Display shells in a box frame or printer's drawer. Line the back with felt and glue the shells in place.

A Beach Glass Trivet (AGES 5 AND UP, WITH HELP)

These are not only fun for children to make but help protect the table from hot plates at mealtime. Trivets make great gifts for adults—a favorite teacher, relative, or friend.

Simple Fun

I can hear the ocean! Hold a conch shell (or any large, coiled univalve type of shell) up to your ear. The shell amplifies the sound of the sea—much as your ear amplifies the sounds it receives.

Simple Fun

Sand is actually tiny fragments of rock, shell, and coral. Try collecting sand from different beaches and see how the samples vary in color and texture.

A disposable pie tin
A piece of felt
Plaster of Paris
An empty coffee can
A stick, for stirring
Cooking oil
Assorted beach glass
Glue

Turn the pie tin upside down and trace a circle on the felt. Cut out the circle, and set aside. Choose enough pieces of beach glass to cover the bottom of the pie tin. Following the directions on the Plaster of Paris container, mix the plaster with water in the coffee tin. Stir until smooth; it should be the consistency of heavy cream. Oil the bottom of the pie tin lightly and pour in the Plaster of Paris until it is about three-quarters of the way full. Carefully arrange the beach glass in the plaster, pressing down any irregular pieces so that the top is flat. (Work quickly, as the plaster will set in a few minutes.) When the plaster is completely hard, carefully cut away the pie tin. Allow the trivet to sit until it is completely dry. Once dry, turn the trivet over and fit the circle of felt onto the bottom, trimming as necessary. Glue felt in place.

Sand Candles   (AGES 5 AND UP, WITH HELP)

We used to make these every year during my childhood in Florida. Summer dinners in the backyard were never complete without the soft glow from our sand candles.

A large bowl or bucket
Damp sand (enough to fill container)
A candle wick
A dowel or pencil
Paraffin wax, or old candles
Coffee tin
A large saucepan
Bits of crayons (optional)

Fill the bowl with damp sand, which acts as the "mold" for the candle. Dig a hole in the sand, the shape and size you want the candle to be. (A starfish pressed inches in the sand makes a wonderful shape.) Fill a clean coffee tin with paraffin wax, and place the tin in the saucepan. Add a few inches of water to the saucepan and melt the paraffin slowly over medium heat. (Add bits of crayon for colors.) Pour the melted wax into the hole; it will harden as it cools.

Carefully remove candle from the hole, and brush off any loose bits of sand. The base may need to be trimmed so that the candle will sit evenly. Candles may stand alone or in a shallow container filled with small shells.

Note: *For a layered effect, simply melt individual colors (add crayons to wax) and pour thin layers of wax. Allow each layer to cool before adding the next color.*

An Ocean Diorama   (AGES 5 AND UP)

Children can turn a shoe box into an underwater adventure! This is especially fun for urban kids after a day at the beach.

> *A shoe box (the larger the better)*
> *Scissors*
> *Construction paper (blue and other underwater colors)*
> *Glue*
> *Assorted crayons, markers, colored pencils*
> *White thread*
> *Tape*
> *Assorted small beach treasures—little shells, starfish, rocks, bits of seaweed, and sand*

Remove the top of the shoe box and cut a small rectangle in the top for a "skylight." Cut a small square in one end of the box for a "peekhole," so children can view their scene. Cut out blue construction paper to fit the wall opposite the peekhole, the two sides, and the bottom of the box. (Kids can draw on the blue pieces of paper before they are glued in place to create background scenery if desired.) Glue or tape the paper in place inside the box. Cover the bottom of the box with sand, tiny shells, bits of coral, or small rocks to emulate the ocean floor. Cut out several small "fish" from the construction paper (children may color these if they want) and tape a short length of white thread to each fish. (Vary the length of

City Watch

Spend the day at the beach! Gather shells and a container of sand for a beachcomber's party. Throw brightly colored beach towels on the table for a tablecloth. Make a centerpiece with the sand comb: Fill a baking tray with a thin layer of sand and make swirls and other designs. Top with any other beach treasures. Now let's party!

KID-SOURCE

The Center for Marine Conservation
1725 DeSales Street, NW
Washington, D.C. 20036
202-429-5609

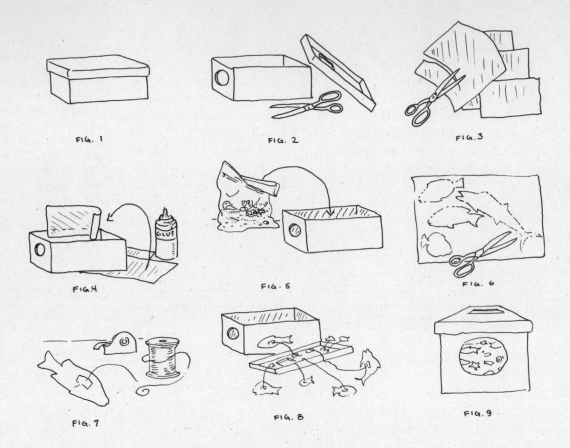

FIG. 1   FIG. 2   FIG. 3

FIG. 4   FIG. 5   FIG. 6

FIG. 7   FIG. 8   FIG. 9

the threads for the best effect.) Tape the other end of the thread to the inside lid of the box. Put the lid on the box, making sure the "skylight" is at the end away from the peekhole, and view the scene. Adjust the placement of the fish and threads as necessary— fish should appear to float over the bottom of the "ocean." (Have some fish close to the peekhole and others at the other end of the box.) Once children are pleased with the arrangement, tape the lid securely to the box, and move to a well-lit area for a good look.

Native American Sand Painting   (Ages 4 and Up)

The Navajo and Hopi tribes of the Southwest make sacred designs from sand and other natural materials to heal the sick. Children can do a simple version by gluing colored sand onto a sheet of sandpaper.

Sand (salt may be substituted)
Powdered tempera paint (or powdered chalk); earth tones are tradi-
tional—white, black, gray, brown, terra-cotta, yellow, and blue
Containers for mixing sand
Shallow containers for holding individual colors of sand
1 sheet of sandpaper
Dark-colored chalk or charcoal
Glue
A small fine-tip brush
Newspaper

If children would like to use sand that they have found, let them sift it through a kitchen strainer to remove any small debris. Tint sand by stirring in a bit of paint or chalk until the desired shade is obtained. Otherwise, colored sand may be purchased. Place the sheet of sandpaper on a work surface that has been covered with newspaper. Some children like to work out their design on paper beforehand. Try to find some books on Native American art at the library. Navajos used many lines to create their designs, which were highly stylized rather than realistic looking. Traditional symbols include:

Long-limbed people representing the Holy People, or gods
The four winds: north, south, east, west
Native American plants: corn, beans, squash, tobacco
The sun and moon
Eagle, snake, feathers
Clouds, rain, thunder, lightning, rainbows
Broken arrow (the symbol for peace)

Draw your design on the sandpaper, using chalk or charcoal. Paint one small area of the design with glue, and sprinkle with sand, using one color of sand at a time. Allow the sand to set for a few minutes. Lift the sandpaper up, tilt, and tap lightly to dislodge any loose bits of sand. (This loose sand may be collected and saved for future use.) Continue working with one color at a time until the design is complete. Allow to dry overnight. Frame the artwork if desired.

The Great Cleanup

After a day at the beach, children can easily see that we share this magnificent resource with other living creatures. From the tiny little periwinkles clinging to the rocks, to the herring gull crying his shrill song as he circles overhead, to the curious little fiddler crab with his comical comings and goings—the beach is teeming with life. Plankton, the microscopic plant and animal life found in the ocean, is so small that it can't be seen with the naked eye, yet is the beginning of the food chain, on which all other sea life depends!

Children can do their share to preserve this delicate ecosystem. Always take your trash with you when you leave the beach. (There's a maxim I grew up with: "Wherever you go, leave it nicer for *you* having been there." My grandmother told me this when I was young and I have passed it on to my children.) Trash left behind not only pollutes the area, but can be fatal to creatures that inhabit the sea—disposable plastic six-pack rings may get caught around the necks of unsuspecting birds and fish, and plastic bags might be ingested by turtles—floating plastic bags look an awful lot like jellyfish, a favorite delicacy of sea turtles!

All over the country kids and adults are helping to keep our coastline and beaches clean. Kids can write to The Center for Marine Conservation for information on the *Coastal Connection* newsletter, which promotes beach clean-up events. If we all lend a hand, we can make a difference!

Adoption Programs

Children can "adopt" a sea turtle or a whale through the following organizations. These programs make great classroom projects or birthday presents.

Adopt a Turtle

The Marinelife Center monitors beaches for sea turtle nests and releases hatchlings that would otherwise not make it on their own. By adopting a turtle, kids can help support their efforts. Adopting Parents receive an individual Certificate of Adoption and the *Turtle Times* newsletter. Adoption for a single turtle is $15.00. Write the

Marinelife Center for more information: The Marinelife Center of Juno Beach, 1200 U.S. Highway One, Loggerhead Park, Juno Beach, FLA 33408.

Adopt a Whale

Kids love the idea of adopting one of these huge cetaceans! Through the International Wildlife Coalition a child can get an official Whale Adoption Certificate, a personal photograph of her whale, and a subscription to *Whalewatch*—a publication that will keep her up to date on her whale's sightings and activity. Write to the Whale Adoption Program for more information. Whale Adoption Project, P.O. Box 388, North Falmouth, MA 02556.

Let's Go Fishin'   (AGES 3 AND UP)

Here's a fun game where kids can "fish" using a magnet. It's the perfect activity after a long day at the beach, when adults need something to entertain the kids before bedtime. This game can be set up in a matter of minutes if you have a magnet on hand and is great for summertime birthday parties too!

A length of string
A dowel or stick
A magnet
Glue gun
Large paper clips
Construction paper
Scissors
A cardboard box (optional)

Tie the string on to one end of the dowel. Attach the magnet to the other end of the string. (Glue the magnet on with a hot glue gun if necessary.) Cut different size fish out of the construction paper (children may color fish, if desired), and attach two large paper clips to the mouth of each one. An "ocean" or "pond" can be made out of a cardboard box. Have the kids decorate all four sides of the box—adding pictures of sea creatures, seaweed, wavy grass, and starfish. Place all of the fish in the box and let the kids try and "catch" one with the magnet.

Good Reading

Harriet Ziefert. *Henry's Wrong Turn*. Boston: Little, Brown, 1989. (Ages 5 to 9)

Wiggly Fish

These are fun for kids to make and eat! Try making them in different shapes as well.

4 cups cold fruit juice
4 envelopes unflavored gelatin
Fish-shaped cookie cutters

Pour 1 cup of juice into a medium-size bowl. Sprinkle the gelatin over the juice and allow to stand for one minute. Boil the remaining 3 cups of juice. Add the gelatin mixture, and stir until well dissolved. Pour into a 9- by 13-inch pan and refrigerate until firm. Using cookie cutters, cut the gelatin into desired shapes.

Note: *Leftover gelatin is great over cottage cheese.*

Away at Camp

Being away at a sleep-over camp during the summer months can be a very exciting time for a child. With their newfound independence comes the chance to meet different people, create life-long friendships, and try out a wide assortment of activities. The transition from home to camp can be a tough one, though—with homesickness, sleepless nights, and no letters or packages at mail call. Here are some ideas to make sure the children in your life are "happy campers"!

Brownies

Made with less sugar than most traditional recipes, these are delicious, and as all-American as summer camp! They pack well and are a great addition to a "care package."

> 6 tablespoons unsalted butter
> 3 squares unsweetened chocolate
> 1⅓ cups sugar
> 3 eggs
> ¼ teaspoon salt
> ¾ cup unbleached flour
> 1 teaspoon vanilla
> ½ cup chopped walnuts (optional)

Preheat the oven to 350°F. Butter a 9-inch-square pan and set aside. Combine the butter and the chocolate together in a saucepan, and stir over low heat until smooth. Remove from the heat and add the eggs, one at a time, stirring well after each addition. Add the sugar, salt, and flour, and stir until just combined.

Simple Fun

Save all of those summer postcards and turn them into a simple wall hanging. Punch holes in the top corners of the postcards and tie them together in a long line with brightly colored yarn. Remind kids to send themselves postcards while away from home. They're a great reminder of a fun summer!

Good Reading

- Jane O'Connor. *Yours Till Niagara Falls*. N.Y.: Scholastic Books, 1982. (Ages 8 to 11)
- Judith Gorog. *No Swimming in Dark Pond and Other Chilling Tales*. N.Y.: Philomel, 1987. (Ages 9 to 13)

Add the vanilla, and stir. Add nuts if desired, and pour mixture into the prepared pan. Bake in the middle of the oven, for about 30 minutes, or until a toothpick comes out clean. Cool on a rack before cutting into squares.

Shipping: Brownies can be individually wrapped in foil or waxed paper or carefully stacked between layers of waxed paper. Cookie tins or shoe boxes are good containers for mailing.

"We Care" Packages

At summer camp, nothing is looked forward to as much as the daily mail. Here are some ideas for letters and packages that say "We love you, we're thinking of you!"

- Letter writing can easily slip for parents during the hectic days of summer. Try keeping a stack of stamped and addressed postcards on the kitchen counter, dinner table, or wherever your family hangs out. Encourage family members, friends, and guests who drop in to take a few minutes to say hello to your campers. Younger kids can make drawings with crayons or markers while meals are being prepared.
- When doing the weekly grocery shopping buy an extra package or two of favorite cookies, crackers, or snacks. Keep a few padded envelopes in the car for easy shipping on the way home.

My Camp Time-Line Scroll   (ALL AGES)

Kids can make a scroll of daily or weekly happenings as a memento of camp. This reminder of summer makes a fun activity at home too. Even toddlers can join in the fun—my three-year-old son made one last summer. He made little scribbles every week, and told me what they stood for as I wrote a sentence or two for him.

A roll of paper (plain white shelf paper works well)
Colorful markers
White glue
Memorabilia—movie ticket stubs, leaves, flowers
A piece of yarn or ribbon

KID-SOURCE

Sealed With a Kiss
P.O. Box 2063
Rockville, MD 20852
800-888-7925
Provides nonfood packages to children at sleep-over camp for $22.50 plus shipping. Items included are fun, age- and sex-appropriate things to do with friends or alone.

Mark off sections of paper every foot or so, label with the date, and reroll. Kids can record the day's or week's happenings in each section as they unroll the paper. Encourage kids to add on any small bits of memorabilia that can be rolled up in the scroll as well. The scroll may be kept rolled up and tied with yarn between entries.

Note: *A Camp Time-Line Scroll makes a great "care package" addition, especially if an adult divides the scroll into sections and labels each with the date and includes an assortment of colorful markers.*

Let's Make an Impression

Kids love the idea of making stamps and creating designs from items at hand—whether summer vegetables and fruits or everyday common household items. Children can start out on paper, making postcards, invitations, and posters. Once they get the hang of it, kids can move on to printing on fabric.

Fruit and Vegetable Prints (AGES 3 AND UP, WITH HELP)

Raid the kitchen to do this project! Be sure to cover your work surface first with several layers of newspaper.

What to look for:

- apples—these make heart shapes when cut in half
- bananas—make concentric circles
- broccoli, cauliflower—create a dappled effect
- carrots, potatoes, and sweet potatoes—can be carved into numerous shapes
- lemons, oranges, grapefruits—cut in half for circles, or in quarters for a wedge shape
- onions—concentric circles or separate into rings for circles of various sizes (make great "eyes")
- string beans—cut in half the long way, with beans still intact
- peppers—cut into rings

Lay out the paper or cardboard to be printed. Kids can use ink pads in various colors or soak individual sponges with paint. (Pie plates and clean styrofoam meat trays come in handy to hold the sponges.) Dress the kids in old clothes, or cover them with old smocks or shirts.

Simple Fun

Children can use their fingers as a stamp! Press a thumb or forefinger into the stamp pad and press against paper. Try making a thumbprint and turning it into a funny face or animal by drawing in features with a fine-tip marker. More adventurous youngsters can try making stamps with their whole hand or foot—though this is best done outside!

Press the "stamps" into the ink pads or sponges, making sure the whole surface of the stamp is covered. Start with lighter colors first. Press the stamp firmly on the paper to create an impression. Overlap colors if desired—just be sure to wash the first color off the stamp, and let the initial color dry, before adding the second color. Younger kids work best with one or two colors. Older kids may like to work in their favorite colors—making monochromatic designs with three or four shades. Add touches of complementary colors for interest, if desired.

Note: *Make letters and numbers backward when cutting out stamps; that way they will print correctly!*

My Chinese Chop   (AGES 8 AND UP, WITH SUPERVISION)

Try making a chop, like the Chinese. Chinese people use a chop as we do our signature. All legal documents, business papers, and checks are signed with a chop. Artists use a chop with red ink to sign works of art. There are eight styles of Chinese calligraphy, and a Chinese person must choose one style and register it with his local government office. Kids can make their own chops by carving their own "marks" on small, flat pieces of potatoes. They can then stamp their own artwork, letters, notes, and books. For a real challenge, try cutting a ring out of a potato and carving the symbol on the flat top. Kids will get a kick out of using their own private marks.

Anything Can Make a Mark   (AGES 3 AND UP)

Once the kids have mastered fruits and vegetables, it's time to raid other parts of the house for items to use as "stamps." Check your supply of recycled and reusable items for ideas too!

- empty paper towel or toilet paper tubes
- empty soda cans
- hair rollers (ask permission first)
- old thread, ribbon spools
- lids to various containers
- wadded pieces of tinfoil, newspaper, and cheesecloth
- potato masher, small mesh strainer

- forks
- soles from old sneakers, shoes
- dry pasta—rotelle (wagon-wheel shape), rotini, and other shapes
- cookie cutters
- old paintbrushes, toothbrushes, hair brushes
- discarded pieces of wood
- old sponges (cut into shapes)

The method is the same as for vegetable stamps.

For a variation, try this on a cardboard tube or soda can: Cut a 14-inch length of yarn or heavy twine. Dip the yarn in Elmer's glue and wind it around the tube or can to create a pattern. Try cutting several pieces of yarn and crisscrossing them to create various effects. Let the glue dry. Press the "soda can stamp" in the paint, being sure to cover all sides of the yarn completely. Roll the can over the paper; the yarn will create a repeating pattern on the paper.

African "Good-bye" Cloth (AGES 8 AND UP)

Older children who have mastered the art of carving potatoes into stamps may wish to try their hands at printing on fabric and making a traditional Adinkra cloth. "Adinkra" is the Ashanti word for "good-bye," and the cloth is the customary dress of the Ashanti tribe of Ghana, West Africa. Generally worn when friends are departing, and at funerals, the cloth is characterized by specific symbols carved from pieces of gourd and stamped within square sections of fabric. (This makes an especially good classroom project.)

> *A piece of fabric*
> *Ruler (for squaring off the lines)*
> *Pen*
> *Potatoes*
> *Carving tools (butter knives, clay-modeling tools)*
> *Black acrylic paint*
> *Sponges*
> *Containers*
> *Rit fabric dye (bright colors are best)*

Simple Fun

Make a traditional Ashanti headdress, known as a *Gele*. Cut a piece of fabric about 3 feet long and 12 inches wide. Twist the fabric into a rope and coil around the child's head. Tuck in the loose ends. Works great with a Good-bye cloth!

Divide the fabric into squares using the ruler and pen. Carve a symbol into the flat side of a potato half. Soak the sponge with the black paint. Press each potato stamp into the paint-filled sponge and stamp each square of the fabric. Re-ink the stamp after each impression is made for the best results. (Children may use the same symbol within each square, or try a combination of symbols for a different effect.)

When all of the fabric has been stamped, allow it to dry completely. Heat-set the designs by ironing the cloth with a warm iron. (Adults only, please.) Children may leave their fabric white as the male tribesmen do, or dye it with fabric dye before stamping, as the Ashanti women do.

Dog-Day Amusements

The dog days of summer are the days both child and adult dread—they are the hottest, most miserable days of the entire season. Days when the children are bored, cranky, and longing for something fun to do and when adults are feeling helpless, irritable, and at their wits' end as to how to keep the kids happy and entertained. Welcome to our Dog-Day Amusements! We've put together some fast, and not-so-fast, solutions to keep the kids in your life busy and content.

Scratch Pictures   (AGES 3 AND UP)

Many people will remember these from their own childhood—they're fun and easy to make. Using a variety of brightly colored crayons, completely cover a piece of construction paper. Make sure the colors are on thick. Paint the entire paper with a black acrylic paint and let it dry completely. "Scratch" a picture on the paper, using a key, a coin, wooden stick, or an unsharpened pencil. Wherever the paint has been scratched off, the color will show through. Frame each child's best picture and hang it on the wall!

The Marble Garage Game   (AGES 3 AND UP)

My son thinks that the box in this game looks like a "garage," so that's what we have named it! Let an older child who can add a column of figures serve as scorekeeper. All you need is a rectangular-shaped box and a handful of marbles to play.

Remove the lid from the box and set the box (with the open side facing down) on your work surface. Draw several openings, of various widths (1 inch wide, 1½ inches wide, 1¾ inches wide,

THE DOG DAYS OF SUMMER

During the hottest days of summer (early June to mid September) the Dog Star—Sirius—is visible on the horizon. These sweltering days came to be known as the "Dog Days" of summer.

2 inches wide), along the bottom edge of one of the sides of the box. Cut out each opening with scissors. Each opening is worth a certain number of points, depending on the difficulty involved. Label each opening with the following point system: 6 points (1-inch opening), 4 points (1½-inch opening), 2 points (1¾-inch opening), and 1 point (2-inch opening). Place the box on the floor (with the open side facing down) and have the first player sit about 4 feet back from the openings. Each player starts with four marbles. Kids may roll one marble at a time or play all of them at once if desired. Let each player shoot all of their marbles before the next person's turn. Children may simply test their skill at shooting marbles through the various openings for a noncompetitive version or may keep score and see who reaches 60 points first. As the children's skill improves, try having them move farther away from the box.

Newspaper Buildings   (AGES 4 AND UP)

My children and I have made wonderful villages from newspaper tubes! All you need are a stack of old newspapers and some everyday items to make buildings, silos, airplanes, and rafts. Once assembled, kids can turn their creations into any number of scenes—your town, a Wild West town, a farm, an airport, a harbor. Add little cars, figures, and props for hours of fun!

Newspaper
White glue
Pen
Ruler
Scissors
Play accessories

Lay several layers of newspaper on the table and fold them in half. Cut 5- by 14-inch strips out of the newspaper. Roll the individual strips around a pencil. Remove the pencil and glue the loose end of the newspaper roll down. Set aside to dry. Continue rolling and gluing tubes of newspaper until you have enough to make a building of some sort. (Make some tubes 2½ by 14 inches so kids can make doorways and windows in their buildings too.) Have kids glue tubes together to make the desired shape. Use the smaller

Simple Fun

Help! There's no paint in the house! Here's a recipe for Paint-in-a-Pinch: Combine 1 big squirt of white glue, ¼ teaspoon water, and 1 drop of food coloring. Be sure to wash brushes well after use.

tubes wherever you want a door or a window. Kids can place buildings on a large piece of posterboard for a more realistic setting. Color in grass, streets, a pond, and other features, as desired. Tubes may also be painted solid colors before construction begins.

Sweet Frames

(AGES 4 AND UP)

We make these candy picture frames for birthday parties, though children can make them any time! Be prepared to have the kids eat some of their supply of candy, so buy a little extra! These are great frames for summer pictures—try shooting a roll of Instamatic film or let the kids clown around with a disposable camera. Most film processing stores can have pictures back to you within one hour.

> *Assorted wrapped candy (hard candies work best and don't melt as much)*
> *Glue*
> *Cardboard picture frames*
> *A photograph or drawing*

Pile candy into bowls and let kids glue an assortment around the edge of the frame. Add glitter and bits of ribbon if desired. Allow to dry before framing a picture.

Sewing Cards (AGES 3 AND UP)

This was my introduction to sewing. My mother used to save pretty pictures from old magazines and calendars to use for Sewing Cards. This simple project is a wonderful way to introduce children to the world of needlework. It's also a great way to put some of the kids' smaller works of art to good use!

A picture
Medium-weight paper for backing (postcard or scrap paper, at least the same size as picture)
Glue
Tape
Hole puncher
A long piece of string for sewing

Cut the picture to a manageable size. Spread a thin layer of glue onto the back of the picture and press onto the backing paper. Allow to dry, and trim the edges as needed. Punch holes along the edge of the picture, spacing them at least an inch apart from each other. Cut a length of string long enough to lace around the entire edge of the picture. Knot one end of the string, and wrap a small piece of tape around the other end (like the tip of a shoelace) for ease in sewing. Let children lace the string in and out of the holes.

Note: *My mother used to make paper dolls out of sturdy paper and let me "sew" on their clothes. You can make similar dolls out of sturdy paper by punching holes at the top of the shoulders and along the outside of the torso. Cut an assortment of clothes from paper (lay the doll on the paper and trace around the outline of the body): dresses, shirts, skirts, and pants. Let children color the clothes with crayons or markers. Align the clothes with the doll and punch holes in the clothing that correspond to the holes in the doll. Let children "dress" dolls by sewing on various outfits. We used to also cut out hats and shoes and sew these on with one or two stitches.*

Good Reading

- Linda Gong and Susan Echaore-Yoon. *Basic Sewing.* Wichita, KS: Janus Books, 1989. (Ages 11 and up)
- Cheryl Arrants and Dennis Arrants. *Thimbelina & the Notion Parade.* Bellevue, WA: Arrants and Assoc., 1983. (Ages 5 to 9)

My Postmark Collection (AGES 5 AND UP)

Kids love collecting things—from shells to minerals, leaves, pressed flowers, coins, stamps, baseball cards, and postmarks. Postmarks?! Yes, here's an unusual hobby that will send kids off each day to check the mail. Make a simple book out of construction paper: Cut sheets of construction paper in half and punch three holes along one long side. Lace the pages together with yarn or string and label each page with the name of a state. Adults can save envelopes from the daily mail and let kids cut out and paste the postmarks on the appropriate pages. Try labeling one page "Other Countries" and see how many foreign postmarks kids can collect by the end of the summer. Try trading postmarks with friends, relatives, and neighbors. Suggest making a "Postmarks Wanted" sign and hanging it in your local post office or mailing company.

A Box of Memories   (AGES 3 AND UP, WITH HELP)

Kids can preserve the highlights of their summer (or any season) with this fun project. Shoe boxes work well for holding mementos—let kids paint the outside of the boxes and lids, or cover them with decorative paper. Save some of the objects to glue onto the boxes. Label each box with the child's name and the date. Kids will find it fun to start one every summer, and to look back on previous years. It helps them recall the best of times! My daughter Lauren started making these when she was four, and we have a stack of them on her closet shelf. It's fun to look through them as a family. A box of memories might include:

- Photos (especially those taken by child)
- Ticket stubs to concerts, sports events, amusement parks, movies
- Rocks, shells, small found treasures
- Travel mementos—tickets, maps, subway tokens
- Restaurant memorabilia—coasters, menus, placemats, napkins
- Drawings, letters, postcards
- A list of the summer's favorite foods, friends, songs, videos, books (have kids date the items on the list)

Create a Home Restaurant   (AGES 3 AND UP)

A restaurant of your very own can turn dinner, or any other meal, into a fun learning experience for kids. Look through cookbooks together and dream up a meal—try to stick to no-fuss recipes that won't be too challenging. (Or better yet, for real easy summer living, order a take-out meal that corresponds to the theme the kids have chosen!) Encourage children to think up a name for their restaurant, and make a sign, menu, and placemats. Let them set the table and pick out the background music to set the right mood! Raid the closets for classic white shirts and black pants or skirts for "servers" to wear. Give children a pen and a pad of store-bought restaurant order forms so they can take orders and give you a bill. (Fold a white napkin and let the server hang it over his arm for added effect.) Some restaurant themes to consider are: a pizza parlor, a BBQ joint, a diner, a bagel shop, or a fancy French restaurant. Try an ice cream parlor for dessert! Kids will take a real interest in meals, grocery shopping, and cooking as a result.

Nana's Clothesline Game   (AGES 3 AND UP)

This is a game my mother uses to entertain her grandchildren during long, hot summer days on Cape Cod. We seldom use the dryer in the summer months, opting instead for the fresh smell of clothes dried in the summer sun. There's invariably a lone sock left flapping in the breeze, which has somehow lost its mate! I imagine this spurred my mother's imagination, for soon my children's boredom lifted with the invention of Nana's Clothesline Game!

Gather all the old, stray socks together as well as a good supply of clothespins. Search the house for some objects to hide in the toe of the socks. Try a small spoon, a large paper clip, a nail, an apple, small scissors, a palm-size book, a hair comb, a shell, a pencil or anything else you think will work. Put one item in the toe of a sock, and secure to the clothesline with a clothespin. Let each child take a turn feeling the sock and guessing what is inside. (Older kids can take turns feeling all the socks and writing down the answers. Younger children will enjoy blurting out their guesses until they figure it out. Hints are allowed for the younger ones.) You can make this noncompetitive or award a prize to the child who gets the most correct answers.

A Roadside Stand (AGES 5 AND UP)

Enterprising youngsters can get out of the summer doldrums, and turn a profit as well, by setting up a roadside stand. Kids can sell anything from lemonade to trail mix in bags or excess produce from a summer garden. All they need is a product, a table, a pen and paper for keeping a record of sales, and a box full of coins to make change with. Making a sign for their stand can be a fun project. Make sure kids wear hats and sunblock to protect them from the hot summer sun. Profits could be put into a special savings account, and the amount might be matched by an adult as an added incentive.

Piggy Bank (AGES 4 AND UP, WITH HELP)

A plastic gallon jug becomes a wonderful bank in this easy project. This pig is a great addition to the previous activity and makes good use out of common household items.

A clean gallon jug
An empty egg carton
A cardboard tube (from toilet paper or paper towels)
A 1 ¾- to 2-inch button with 2 holes (preferably pink)
Pink and black construction paper
Glue
Scissors
Pencil and pen

Cut four individual sections from the egg carton for legs. Lay the jug on its side and glue the legs in place, making sure the pig can stand. Cut 3 inches off one end of the cardboard tube for the nose. Glue the button onto one end of the tube. Glue the other end of the tube (the open end) over the spout of the jug. Cut triangles out of construction paper for ears and glue in place. (Bend the tops of the ears for a whimsical touch.) Cut eyes out of paper and glue on the pig. Make eyelashes by fringing a short strip of paper, and a curly tail by wrapping a thin strip of paper around a pencil tightly for a few moments. Glue in place. Have an adult cut a slit in the top of the pig for coins.

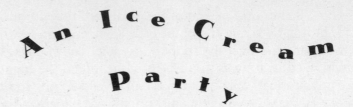

An Ice Cream Party

Ask most kids what they think of when summer comes to mind, and they will invariably mention ice cream! Summer and ice cream have been synonymous in the United States for well over two hundred years, with ice cream parlors in full swing by the late 1800s. Here are two scrumptious recipes to get your Ice Cream Party into full swing. Add store-bought ice cream in your favorite flavors, jimmies, sprinkles, and whipped cream for an instant party.

Butterscotch Sauce

This is sinfully rich and a real kid-pleaser when served warm over vanilla ice cream.

¾ cup light brown sugar
⅓ cup light corn syrup
4 tablespoons (½ stick) unsalted butter
½ cup heavy cream

Combine all ingredients in a medium-size pan and bring to a boil over medium-high heat. Boil for 5 minutes. Remove from heat and stir vigorously for about 30 seconds. Cool slightly before serving. Yields about 1½ cups.

The Best Fudge Sauce

The name says it all!

3 tablespoons unsalted butter, cut into bits
⅓ cup sugar
⅓ cup dark brown sugar, firmly packed

½ cup Dutch process cocoa
⅓ cup heavy cream

Combine all ingredients in a medium-size saucepan and stir over medium heat until the butter has melted. Turn heat down to low, and continue to stir mixture, scraping the sides of the pan as necessary, until all of the sugar has melted. Serve at once, or allow to cool slightly. Makes 1 cup of sauce.

Note: *Sauce may be refrigerated and reheated slowly in a double boiler.*

The Signs

Your guide to keeping children
in tune with the season.

A WALK IN THE WOODS

Take kids for a walk on the wild side—of the
Autumn woods! Search out leaves and seeds for
rubbings and pressed-leaf placemats. Make a
Native American pine needle doll and a
walnut "Skier"!

GRANDPARENTS' DAY

Honor these most valuable members of
childhood with some "multi-generational"
amusements and family pastimes. Take Grandma
or Grandpa to the kitchen and stir up some
homemade Buttermilk Ranch Dressing—a
child's staple!

THE LITTLE "FALL" GARDENER

Keep young gardeners busy during the winter
months with dried flowers for a Mini Standard,
fragrant Sachets, and an herbal moth repellent.
Bookworms can make simple pressed-flower
bookmarks. Draw up a Bulb Treasure Map—a
handy guide for locating each year's
spring-blooming bulbs!

SCHOOL DAYS

Design Cool Cover-Ups for schoolbooks. Try
some fun art projects for Marbled Paper and
Blender Paper! Feed Me! Keep kids happy and
"nutrition-wise" with some great tips and a
child-pleasing Turkey Meatloaf.

APPLES

Pick a bushel of apples for Apple Cake and make
Appleheads for homemade dolls. Flick an apple
seed in our Apple Seed Olympics—just like they
did in Grandpa's Day!

# of Autumn

HALLOWEEN

Send shivers down children's spines with some fun holiday pursuits—craft Ghosts, a Ghost Tree, and edible Monster Mitts! Roll marbles for Spiderweb Placemats, turn a chestnut into a giant Cobweb, and learn some Spook-tacularly silly jokes! There's a Magic Broomstick Brew to try, and tasty chocolate Black Cat cookies to bake. Find your way through the Crazy Mixed-Up Web game, and try two activities that call on "divining" spirits of this autumn night!

THANKSGIVING

Give thanks to those who mean the most to you with these cherished family traditions. Make this Thanksgiving a standout with Pass the Apple, Holiday Bingo, and two yummy recipes—Cheese Fondue and Gingerbread with Cinnamon Whipped Cream!

JUST BETWEEN US

Keep them guessing with our Secret Codes! Learn Pig Latin, how to make Invisible Ink, and a brain-teasing Computer Code. Keep your communications with friends top secret with the Greek Spiral Code, the Tic-Tac-Toe Code, and Flash! a flashlight signal game. Pass on some silly Bits of Nonsense—riddles and poems that have stood the test of time. End your one-of-a-kind letters with our Silly Sign-Offs and tongue-twisters!

YOUNG HEARTS AND HANDS

Multicultural fun like Get to Know Another Country puts kids in touch with their world. Make a difference with some community and global actions!

AUTUMN AFTERNOONS

Beat those fall blahs with Bicycle Mania, Homemade Flubber, a Tin Lantern, and "Socks"—the hobbyhorse!

AUTUMN WONDERS

WITH THE ARRIVAL OF cooler weather, children trade their carefree ways for school days, sports practice, and familiar routines! All of nature hunkers down as the earth prepares for winter:

- The days grow shorter as the sun sets earlier and lower in the sky
- Nights become cool as the moon rises golden and full. The earth pulls further away from the sun
- The woods rustle with the sound of falling leaves
- Cool breezes drift by, richly perfumed with the incense of burning leaves
- The hawthorn bush hangs heavy with its gift of scarlet fruit
- Bird nests lay empty as swallow, robin, lark, and bluebird take to the sky and head south
- The goldenrod, aster, cockscomb, and witch hazel burst into bloom
- Storms and hurricanes build in the Gulf Stream and head north
- Buckeyes ripen, nuts and cones drop, and the milkweed fluff floats by on the wind
- The constellations Cassiopeia, Perseus, and Romeda twinkle together in the autumn sky
- Beavers busily gather branches from the aspen and alder
- Bats seek refuge from the cold in hollow trees and caves

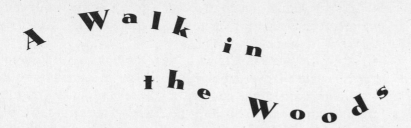

A Walk in the Woods

It's the beginning of autumn and the woods are bustling with activity as both animals and plants prepare for winter. Children delight in the seasonal happenings, as all of nature gets ready for the onset of cold weather. Whether you live in the city or the country, set aside a day to explore the woods with the children in your life—observe area wildlife, collect fallen treasures, and enjoy the brisk temperatures this time of year brings.

Check with your local parks and recreation department for any area nature preserves; protected acreage generally has trails to walk on, and often provides information on local wildlife and plants you are apt to see. (Before entering any wooded area children should always wear bright colors, walk with an adult, and carry a compass.) If you want to walk on private land make sure you have written permission from the owner, and carry it with you. As an added precaution on private land, find out when the local hunting season opens and be sure to stay out of the woods during those weeks.

Children who enter the woods quietly will be rewarded as they become a part of this busy world not often seen by humans. Stop every so often along your journey—you may be fortunate enough to see

- Squirrels busily darting back and forth, their cheeks comically bulging with nuts, seeds, and berries
- Wild turkeys foraging for acorns on the ground
- Birds and animals greedily feasting on wild berries ripening on the bushes
- Bees hastily sipping the last bit of nectar from blossoms
- Wasps busily preparing for the next generation—leaving egg galls on the limbs of trees

Simple Fun

Rake leaves into a big pile and let children jump in them! Play "leaf limbo"— balance a long stick on top of two level piles of leaves. Have kids crawl under, belly up, without touching the stick!

Good Reading

- Elsa Beskow. *Christopher's Harvest Time.* Edinburgh: Floris Books, 1992. (Ages 3 to 8)
- Claude Clement. *The Voice of the Wood.* N.Y.: Dial Books, 1989. (Ages 8 and up)
- Alvin Tresselt. *Autumn Harvest.* N.Y.: Lothrop, Lee and Shepard, 1951. (Ages 6 to 9)

Simple Fun

Younger kids can make a simple Leaf Rubbing! Tape several leaves face down on paper. Top the leaves with another piece of paper. Rub over the leaves with a crayon to create a "leaf print."

LEAF FOLKLORE

• If the ash shows its leaves before the oak, buckets of rain will fall!
• If you catch a falling oak leaf before it touches the ground, you'll get through the winter without a single cold.
• If a leaf shows its underside, it's a sign of rain.

• Monarch butterflies gliding by on their way south
• Geese honking greetings to each other as they migrate to warmer climates; their signature flight patterns make black chevrons in the sky
• Elk (in the western United States) moving to the lower valleys or white tail deer nibbling on the last of summer's bounty
• In many parts of the country, if you're very lucky you might catch a glimpse of the bald eagle. Salmon return from the Pacific Ocean during the autumn, and the eagle (as well as the bear) feed on the fish—considering this quite a delicacy!

THE FALLING LEAVES

Ask most children what changes the woods go through in autumn and they are most likely to tell you first about the colorful leaves. It's true, with a brilliant burst of color the leaves of autumn bid farewell to summer and reward us with a rainbow of hues—from the golden yellow aster, to the wine-red sumac, the scarlet maple, pale yellow mulberry, bright yellow witch hazel, orange-red sassafras, and the purple sweet gum—each tree glows with its own signature shade. Once the leaf reaches the ground it begins to decay and enrich the soil, and becomes a haven for growing mushrooms, toadstools, countless insects, and small woodland creatures. With a large oak tree alone having more than 250,000 leaves, it's soon apparent how important trees are to the woodland ecosystem!

Leaf Rubbing   (AGES 5 AND UP)

Children will enjoy gathering leaves for this and the next project. Start out by rubbing one leaf. Kids can try rubbing pieces of bark and other bits of textured plant matter as well once they gain experience.

*Newspapers
Ink (water-based printer's ink works well)
Spoon
A flat container with shallow sides*

Brazer (an ink roller with a handle)
Paper (newsprint works well)
Leaves, bark, etc.

Cover your work surface with a protective layer of newspaper. Pour a few spoonfuls of ink into the container and roll the brazer through the ink to coat it well. Place a leaf on the newspaper. Roll the brazer over the top of the leaf, inking it completely. Lay a piece of paper down on the work surface, place the leaf (inked side down) on the paper, and cover with a new sheet of paper. Press the top sheet down firmly with your hands. (You can also roll a rolling pin over the top.) Lift the top piece of paper carefully, and allow the print to dry.

Leaf Playmates (AGES 4 AND UP)

Native American children made dolls out of pine needles—usually from the Norway pine or the red pine, which had longer needles. Cut off a cluster of needles and trim some shorter needles for the arms. If the bottoms are cut straight across, the dolls can stand up. Let kids try to balance them on a pie tin and make them "dance" without falling over. Chippewa children used to do this on pieces of birch bark.

Autumn Walk Placemats (AGES 4 AND UP, WITH HELP)

Children will love gathering different colors and types of leaves for this project. A long runner makes a delightful addition to the holiday table!

Waxed paper
Assorted fall leaves
Ruler
Pencil
Steam iron
Pinking shears or scissors

Cut the waxed paper into desired lengths (18 inches long is good for a placemat, 36 inches and longer for a runner). Have the children arrange the leaves face up on the waxed paper. Place another

Good Reading

Morteza E. Sohi. *Look What I Did With a Leaf!* N.Y.: Walker and Company, 1993. (Ages 3 and up)

Simple Fun

Take a Leaf Walk. Bring along a leaf identification guide and see if kids can match the leaves they find to the ones in the book. Play a silly game, and see who can collect the most leaves while holding their breath! Native American children did this with ferns!

piece of waxed paper the same size as the first on top, and cover with a piece of newspaper. Set the steam iron on a low setting, and press gently to seal. (Ironing should be done by an adult, or an older child with close adult supervision.) Trim the waxed paper as necessary—pinking shears give a nice decorative border to the finished mat.

Good Reading

Eric Carle. *The Tiny Seed.* Saxonville, MA: Picture Book Studio, 1987. (Ages 3 to 8)

A Finder's Search

(AGES 3 AND UP)

Take the children on a seed search. Let one of the children drag an old sock or nylon stocking behind her as she walks. At the end of their walk all kinds of seeds, burs, and whatnot will be stuck to the fabric. Kids can then have a field day identifying what they've caught!

• Glue individual seeds on index cards and have children try to name them. Let them use a seed catalogue or reference books from the library to help name each one. (Local nurseries or botanical gardens can help with tough ones!)

• Try planting some of the seeds that they find. Scatter the seeds on layers of damp paper toweling till sprouted, then place in potting soil, and mist to keep moist. These are fun for kids to put on the kitchen windowsill and check on each morning after breakfast.

Milkweed Pods (AGES 3 AND UP, WITH SUPERVISION)

One of the most fun treasures to be found in the woods is the pod of the milkweed. Long ago children called the individual seeds a "wish fairy." The canoe-shaped pods burst open in the fall and the seeds, with their parachute-like tufts, float through the air. Children used to catch the "wish fairies" in the air, make wishes, and let them go. If a seed regained flight, your wish would come true. If the seed fell to the ground, the wish would not come true.

Note: *Pods also make great miniature canoes and float in the water.*

Simple Fun

Make a Mapleseed Dragonfly! Roll a small bit of green felt into a narrow cylinder. Attach two maple seeds as wings with a dab of glue, and two tiny black seeds (or beans) for eyes.

Simple Fun

Make a Jaunty Skier! All you need are an acorn (with a cap), a walnut, a wooden craft stick, and a scrap of red felt. Glue the acorn head on to the walnut body and allow to dry. (Sandwiching a tiny snip of felt between the two nuts helps with gluing.) Snap the craft stick in half and sand the ends smooth to make 2 skis. Glue each ski in place at the base of the walnut. Cut a 4- by ½-inch piece of felt, fringe the ends, and glue around the neck for a warm scarf! Makes a great Christmas ornament.

The Little "Fall" Gardener

Come autumn, young gardeners are busy picking and enjoying the last of the vegetables and fruits of the season. The joys of past seasons can be captured, however, as children learn to preserve choice flowers, seed pods, and grasses from nature.

Drying Flowers (AGES 5 AND UP, WITH HELP)

Children who want to dry some of their own flowers should gather them on a warm clear morning when their moisture content is low and before the afternoon sun has made them droopy. Arm the children with baskets and scissors, and advise them to choose flowers that are not yet fully open as they will open further during drying.

The Air Dry Method

Have kids pull the leaves off of the lower portions of the stems. Tie the branches together with twine or secure with a rubber band. Find a dark, dry location—an attic or large closet works well. Hang, in bunches of 6 to 8, upside down from the crosspiece of a wooden or heavy plastic hanger. Be sure there is lots of space for proper air circulation. Depending on the variety, flowers will be dry in 10 days to 6 weeks, when petals are slightly brittle to the touch.

Here are two additional methods we use to dry flowers from the autumn garden when there are individual blossoms whose shape must be retained.

Cornmeal Preservative

2 parts cornmeal
1 part powdered Borax

Simple Fun

Let children put their garden "to bed." Start a compost pile with all the leftover plants and dead brush. Have kids sprinkle a "cover crop" (available at your local garden center) of seeds over the garden to improve the soil.

A stationery box or shoe box
Fresh flowers

Mix cornmeal and powdered Borax together. Cover the bottom of the box with a 1-inch layer of the mixture. Cut the flowers, leaving 1-inch stems, and lay face-down in the mixture. Gently spread the petals flat, being sure to leave space between each blossom. Cover the flowers with an additional 1 inch of preservative. Place the lid on the box and store in a cool, dry spot without disturbing for a few days. Children may then check their flowers. Some flowers will dry quicker than others, though most will be ready in 1 to 4 weeks. Carefully remove and use in any dried-flower project.

Baked Sand Method

This method produces dried flowers within a matter of hours and is similar to the technique used in India to dry roses.

Fresh flowers
Large baking pan
3 quarts of clean sand (best purchased from a garden center)
Wire mesh strainer
Soft brush

Make sure the flowers are completely dry, as any dew will cause unattractive brown spots. Cut stems to 1 inch. Preheat the oven to 170°F. Spread 1 inch of sand in the baking pan and arrange the flowers, face up, with the stems buried in the sand. Carefully spread the petals and sift sand over the top of the arrangement with the strainer. Place the pan in the oven and bake for 2 hours. Check periodically, as some flowers dry faster than others. Do not allow flowers to darken. Flowers should feel a bit brittle. Carefully remove the flowers from the sand and lay flat on newspaper to cool. Brush sand off the blossoms with a soft brush.

   Non-oven method. Flowers may also be dried in an airtight metal or plastic container. Place in a dry, slightly warm location for about 5 days. Metal boxes may be placed on a radiator for 2 to 3 days.

   Longer stems can be added to dried flowers by attaching florist's wire up through the blossom: Make a tiny hook on the protruding end and then pull down back through the flower until firmly attached. Flowers may then be stored by inserting into a piece of Oasis until needed.

Flowers that are best suited to the non-oven method are: roses (4 days), delphinium, larkspur, zinnia (3 days), hollyhock, dahlia, and marigold (5 days).

A Mini Standard (Ages 5 and Up)

Children will enjoy making these lovely dried flower topiaries for their room or to give as gifts.

> *Styrofoam ball, 2 to 3 inches in diameter*
> *Dried flower florets*
> *Glue*
> *Stem material—a carved wooden knitting needle, cinnamon sticks, or*
>   *thin birch branch*
> *A small clay pot*
> *Small stones*
> *Dried flower Oasis*
> *Moss*
> *Velvet ribbon*

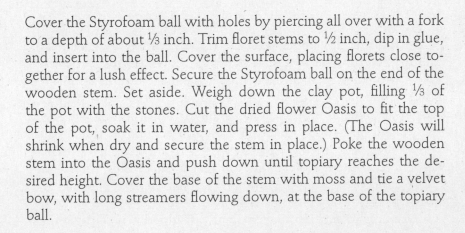

Cover the Styrofoam ball with holes by piercing all over with a fork to a depth of about ⅓ inch. Trim floret stems to ½ inch, dip in glue, and insert into the ball. Cover the surface, placing florets close together for a lush effect. Secure the Styrofoam ball on the end of the wooden stem. Set aside. Weigh down the clay pot, filling ⅓ of the pot with the stones. Cut the dried flower Oasis to fit the top of the pot, soak it in water, and press in place. (The Oasis will shrink when dry and secure the stem in place.) Poke the wooden stem into the Oasis and push down until topiary reaches the desired height. Cover the base of the stem with moss and tie a velvet bow, with long streamers flowing down, at the base of the topiary ball.

Garden Sachets (AGES 5 AND UP)

Children can sew sachets from small scraps of fabric and fill them with a variety of herbal and floral mixtures. Use a combination of moth-repelling herbs for protecting woolens—lavender, rosemary, southernwood, thyme, mint, tansy, wormwood, and santolina. Rosebuds, lemon verbena, violet, chamomile, mint, sweet pea, and scented geranium are all lovely and impart a delicate aroma to clothing and papers. Let children sniff the various dried flowers and make a combination of their choosing. Tied with satin ribbon, they are wonderful for storing with a variety of articles:

- hand-knit sweaters and winter woolens
- children's clothing
- doll clothes, doll house
- a wooden chest full of dress-up clothes
- towels, sheets, and quilts
- writing paper, cards, wrapping paper

Mix the dried petals and blossoms together in a large glass or ceramic bowl. Add 2 to 3 drops of lavender, rose, or other suitable aromatic oil (available at many bath and natural foods stores) and place in a covered cookie tin. Allow to mellow in a cool, dark spot for about a week. Let the children shake the tin daily to further blend the fragrances. When blended, fill the sachet bags and place where desired. For a no-sew version, fabric squares can be cut with pinking shears, and a tablespoon or two of sachet mixture placed in the center. Bring the four corners together and tie with ribbon. Antique lace or print hankies work well too—let kids pick out their favorites at yard sales and thrift shops. Small sachets filled with a mixture of nutmeg, cloves, and cinnamon give off a spicy aroma and make great gifts around the holidays. We tuck a few in boxes of Christmas ornaments too!

Simple Fun

Make a pressed-flower bookmark. Cut two 2- by 7-inch pieces of waxed paper. Lay flowers and leaves on one piece of paper in a pleasing arrangement, and glue in place. Top with the other piece of paper. Set an iron to low, and press the two pieces of waxed paper together. Trim the edges with pinking shears for a pretty border.

Mom's Sweater-Saving Mix (AGES 4 AND UP, WITH CLOSE SUPERVISION)

When we lived on eastern Long Island we raised our own sheep and sent the wool to Maine to be spun into yarn. I knitted many sweaters over the years, thanks to the helpful guidance and patience of my "knitting coach" and good friend, Ann Bellows. Ann is legendary in the Hamptons for her beautiful hand-knit sweaters, often made from homespun wool. This is the mixture I use in sachets to protect our family's woolens.

> 3 ounces assorted moth-repelling herbs (see page 201)
> ¼ cup whole cloves
> 2 cinnamon sticks, crushed (place inside towel and crush with hammer)
> 1 ounce cedar shavings

Combine all the ingredients. Allow aromas to blend by placing in a paper bag and storing in a dark place for a week before needed. Fill the sachets and place among woolens.

Pressed Flowers (AGES 4 AND UP, WITH HELP)

Children may not want to dry all of their flowers, and prefer to save a few to be pressed. Collect flowers and leaves. Place between the pages of a heavy book and leave undisturbed for one week. Carefully remove the pressed material; the edges will be very brittle, so handle with care.

Spring-Flowering Bulbs (AGES 4 AND UP, WITH HELP)

Children can plant bulbs in autumn for a welcome show of color the following spring. Children are often dubious that something that looks as unattractive as a papery-looking old onion can magically turn into a beautiful flower with the onset of warm weather! But, armed with fall catalogues of spring-flowering bulbs, pen and paper, and enthusiasm, they are soon won over. Toward the end of August most garden centers and hardware stores offer a variety of bulbs. This is a fun after-school or weekend project that can be done in stages, as planting can continue throughout autumn until the ground has frozen. Try planting some of the more unusual varieties in addition to the tried and true. Select bulbs that bloom at different times for a lasting display of color.

All-Time Favorites

Old standbys include tulips, hyacinths, crocuses, daffodils, snowdrops, grape hyacinths, irises, narcissi, and allium. Look for unblemished bulbs with no soft spots. It's best to plant your bulbs at once, though they may be stored for a short time in a paper bag in a cool and dry place.

Best Locations

Bulbs do best in partial shade and a well-drained soil. The easiest method is with a bulb-planter and a dibber, two tools that will make planting easier. Mix up a large bucket of compost, peat moss, and sand. Work it into the soil wherever you plan to plant your bulbs and where the soil needs improving. We dig a trench first, work in the soil, and then randomly place the bulbs in the soil. Nature didn't intend bulbs to be lined up like soldiers, so encourage the kids to throw handfuls of bulbs into the prepared beds. Make sure the pointed side is up, and leave at least 3 inches between small bulbs and 5 inches between larger ones. All bulbs come with planting instructions, though a good rule of thumb is to plant them twice as deep as their diameter. Have some bulb fertilizer or bone-meal on hand and apply according to directions. Cover the bulbs, tamping the soil down carefully, and water thoroughly.

Bulb Treasure Map   (AGES 5 AND UP)

Drawing a Treasure Map is fun for kids and will help them remember what they planted and where they put it! Buy an inexpensive ring-binder notebook and have kids draw a map(s) of the location, noting buildings and established bedding areas, using colored pens, crayons, or pencil marks where the bulbs have been planted. We give each variety a number, such as Tulips—1, and make a key or legend. On the back pages of the notebook label a page for each type of bulb planted. List the variety, date planted, and the variety's corresponding number so kids can easily use their map. Cut out a picture of the flowering bulb and paste or tape it to the page for ease in identification.

Apples

It's autumn and apples are the first fruit that comes to mind this time of year. In fact, October is the official Apple Month! During this harvest season, orchards dot the countryside of the world's largest growers. From the United States to Russia, France, Germany, China, Italy, Poland, and Turkey the trees hang heavy with the red, golden and green fruits. Apple trees, like many trees, are a good barometer of what season it is: In spring the fragrant blossoms of pink and white scent the air. In summer the tree has leafed out—the pale green oval leaves shimmer in the heat. Come autumn, the fruit is ready to pick. Apples left on the ground are quickly eaten by local wildlife—deer, fox, and pheasant join in the feast. With the arrival of winter the tree's twisted and gnarled branches hang empty, silhouetted against the cold sky as the apple tree rests before starting the cycle once again.

Five years after the Pilgrims landed, a minister from Boston planted the first apple orchard in America. By 1644 (only twenty years later) John Endicott, then the governor of the Massachusetts Bay Colony, owned over 500 apple trees! The resourceful Pilgrims put the apple tree to a myriad of uses—the fruit was used in cooking and fed to the livestock, and the tree's wood was fashioned into furniture, barrels, parts for tools, toys for the young, and firewood during those first cold seasons in America.

FAVORITE VARIETIES

- McIntosh. One of the most popular. Bright red, with slightly tangy taste and a crisp and fragrant flesh.
- Red Delicious. Bright red with five telltale bumps at the bottom. Juicy and cream-colored inside.
- Granny Smith. Popular in all parts of the world! Green skin and a tart flesh.
- Cortland. Red skin, and pure white meat. Wonderful eaten raw!
- Golden Delicious. Sweet, with yellow skin.
- Rome Beauty. Red skin, yellow flesh. Stores longer than others—perfect for baking apples.

APPLE PICKING

Autumn is the season to take the children to one of those pick-your-own farms. (Check your local yellow pages or county extension service for information.) Apples are one of the few crops today that are still mostly picked by hand. Before you go, learn the correct way to pick apples. It's very important never to pull an apple off the branch. Instead, hold the apple firmly in your hand while you lift and twist it up and away from the tree. This way new buds will form in the spring.

Once you've gotten your bushel of apples home the fun begins! Not only are apples used in more ways than any other fruit (applesauce, apple butter, apple cider, apple vinegar, and apple juice, as well as many tasty dishes such as apple crisp, apple pandowdy, apple pie, apple cake, and apple turnovers), this autumn classic can also entertain children for hours! Stored properly (apples like it cool—a cellar, storage room, or your refrigerator if you have space), your harvest should last you through winter and into spring if you haven't eaten them all by then!

IF YOU ARE AN APPLE: FIVE IS THE MAGIC NUMBER!

- Each apple blossom has five petals
- Flowers usually grow in clusters of five
- Apples cut in half cross-wise reveal a five-pointed star

Waldorf Salad

This is one salad children will usually eat without any fuss! It's a snap for little chefs (younger kids will enjoy stirring the ingredients together) and a great fall salad.

> *4 cups unpeeled red apples, cored and cubed*
> *2 cups sliced celery*
> *1 cup walnut pieces, chopped*
> *1 cup sour cream*
> *½ cup mayonnaise*
> *1 teaspoon lemon juice*

Place the apples, celery, and walnut pieces in a medium-size bowl. In a small bowl blend the sour cream, mayonnaise, and lemon juice together and pour over the apple mixture. Toss until well coated. May be served over chopped lettuce. Makes 8 servings.

Apple Cake

This is quick for breakfast on a school morning, but it's yummy anytime!

> *2 eggs*
> *¾ cup sugar*
> *1 cup canola oil*
> *1¾ cups unbleached flour*

¼ cup whole wheat flour
1 teaspoon baking powder
2 teaspoons cinnamon
¼ teaspoon nutmeg
½ cup walnuts, chopped (optional)
¼ cup applesauce
2½ cups peeled, chopped apples

Preheat the oven to 350°F. Oil and flour a 7- by 10-inch baking pan. In a medium-size bowl combine the eggs and sugar, and beat with a wooden spoon until well blended. Add the oil and mix well. Combine the dry ingredients in a separate bowl, and then add to the egg mixture, beating until well combined. Add the walnuts if desired, and the applesauce and chopped apples. Combine well, and pour into the baking pan. Bake for about 1 hour, or until a toothpick inserted comes out clean. Allow to cool on a rack for about 20 minutes, before cutting. Frost if desired.

Cream Cheese and Honey Frosting

We've used honey in our frosting in honor of the bees! This frosting is also yummy on carrot cake.

> 8 ounces cream cheese
> 2 tablespoons unsalted butter
> ⅛ cup mild-flavored honey
> ½ teaspoon lemon juice
> 2 tablespoons chopped walnuts (optional)

Place the cream cheese and the butter in the bowl of a mixer, and mix until well blended. With the motor running add the honey and lemon juice, and beat until fluffy. Refrigerate the icing until firm. Frost the cake and sprinkle chopped walnuts on top if desired.

Note: *This frosting does best if kept cold; serve frosted cake at once or keep in a refrigerator until needed.*

APPLE PASTIMES

Back in the 1800s children would often spend the whole day with their family at what was then known as an "apple bee." Kids were put to work paring, coring, and cutting apples. After the work was done the children would amuse themselves with various activities. Join us now, as we go back in years, and take a look at some delightful "apple pastimes."

Apple Seed Olympics (AGES 3 AND UP)

Children can place apple seeds on their forefingers and flick them off with the thumb. Place a cup in the middle of the table and let kids try to shoot the seeds into it! See who can get the most seeds in within a certain time frame. Out of doors, kids can draw a chalk line on the sidewalk and see who can flick seeds the farthest.

CONTENTMENT

An apple, a pillow,
A book, and me.
Such simple pleasures,
in the shade of my favorite
tree.

—LAUREN BARTA

HONEYBEE HELPERS

Apple growers depend on the honeybee for cross-pollination: When gathering nectar from an apple blossom, pollen collects on the bee. The bee then transfers that pollen from one blossom to the next. Blossoms that are thus fertilized will become apples. So essential are bees to this process that commercial growers often hire beekeepers to release millions of bees to pollinate their orchards.

APPLE PREDICTIONS

• Apple parings. Toss one continuous apple paring over your right shoulder. When the pare hits the ground it will form the first letter of your future love's name!

• Apple stem. Recite the alphabet while twisting the stem off of an apple. When the stem breaks, the letter you are on is the first letter of your true love's name!

Appleheads (AGES 6 YEARS AND UP, WITH HELP)

It was from the Iroquois tribe of the Northeast that the settlers learned a new use for the apple. For many years the tribal elders had been making doll heads from the native crab apples. Iroquois children treasured these simple toys, and they soon became popular with the pioneer young. Applehead dolls are a simple reminder of a time when toys were lovingly handmade, and possessed a unique character.

Remove all the peel from a large apple, except for a bit at both ends. Make a face on one side of the apple. Create a nose first, by making a ¼-inch-deep triangle with the tip of a toothpick. Emphasize the nose by creating a flat plane on either side of the triangle, for the cheeks. Make the upper lip by cutting a small piece out under the nose. Scoop out two shallow pockets for the eyes. Cut a small slit for the mouth. (As the apple dries, the mouth will open.)

Fine-tune the features with the toothpick or orange stick. The apple will naturally darken as it dries. If you wish to give the doll lighter skin, soak the apple in lemon juice for a few minutes. Fill a

small dish with common salt, and roll the head in it gently. Cut a length of wire and poke one end through the apple, from top to bottom. Bend each end, and hang to dry for several weeks.

Note: *Kids will want to watch the drying process so be sure to hang the head where they can observe the changes taking place. After about 5 days children can further mold their apple's features by pinching and pressing the face with their fingers.*

Bodies can be made of wire: Cut two more lengths of wire— one for the torso, and one for the arms. Fold each of them in half. Put them over each other, then bend ends together at the top to form the neck. Fashion arms and legs out of the four ends of the wires. Secure the wire with masking tape. To fill out the body, cover the wire with pieces of cotton gauze, and wrap with pieces of cloth.

When the head is dry, let children attach it to the body. First enlarge the hole made in the apple for hanging and apply a small amount of glue. Put a small amount of glue on the neck wire, and push the bottom of the applehead onto the figure. Allow to dry. Push cloves into the eye sockets. Hair can be made from yarn, cotton batting, or fleece. Clothing can be sewn from scraps of fabric.

Each dried applehead will have its own character! Children can decide what type of doll they want to make once they study the head for a few minutes. Does it look male or female, young or old? Should the doll wear glasses, or perhaps a hat or jewelry? The possibilities are endless and great fun. My daughter Lauren and I made her applehead into a "grandfather." He had short gray hair, wore glasses, a plaid shirt, and jeans we made from old scraps of faded denim. In his lap sat a cat and a book. We tilted his head, so when sitting in his rocking chair, he appeared to be looking at his cat!

Good Reading

- Gail Gibbons. *The Seasons of Arnold's Apple Tree.* N.Y.: Harcourt Brace Jovanovich, 1984. (Ages 3 to 7)
- Paulette Bourgeois. *The Amazing Apple Book.* N.Y.: Addison-Wesley, 1987. (All ages)

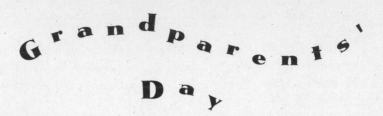

Grandparents' Day

City Watch

Kids in New York City can join Friendly Visiting, 401 Lafayette Street, New York, N.Y. 10003. Children are asked to list their favorite hobbies and are then matched with older individuals with the same interests.

September 12 is the day Americans honor some very important people—grandparents! For those children who don't have any grandparents it's a great day to adopt some. With wonderful tales of what life was like when they were young, grandparents open up children's eyes to the world and give them a sense of belonging. In many parts of the world, where several generations all live under the same roof, it is traditional for grandmothers to pass on stories to the children "so they know where we come from."

Take the opportunity on September 12 to get children together with one grandparent. If this isn't possible, try to schedule some one-on-one time during the upcoming holidays. Even if it's only for an hour or two, this special time spent between generations can leave a lasting impression. Every year when we head north to Cape Cod to visit my mother, our six-year-old daughter, Lauren, asks for "special time alone with Nannie. Just Nannie and me, please."

It's a good idea to overlook some grandparents' small indulgences or flights of fancy when the time the generations have to be together is limited. No real, lasting harm is done after all by allowing Jack to stay up an hour past his normal bedtime (one evening!) or allowing Mia to have ice cream before dinner (just once!).

Try to set up some sort of an activity—looking through an album of family pictures, reading some favorite stories, or cooking something up in the kitchen. This can take the pressure off when kids haven't seen their grandparents for a while and be a great springboard for deeper conversation.

COOKIN' TOGETHER

People usually think of Grandma in the kitchen when it comes time to prepare meals, though some families have a grandpa who shines when it comes time to make pizza, grill on the BBQ, or whip up a family favorite! Older children can enlist the help of a grandparent (or two) to put together a cookbook of family favorites that can be photocopied and shared with family members. With pen and paper in hand, have kids interview relatives and look through old recipe files together. Try inventing some new recipes together too. Here's a salad dressing my daughter loves to make with her Nannie.

Lauren and Nannie's Buttermilk Ranch Dressing

This dressing is loved by kids and grandparents alike! As a dip for raw veggies, a salad dressing over lettuce, or a sauce for steamed vegetables—it's a hit!

> ¾ cup dried onion flakes
> ¼ cup dried parsley flakes
> 2 tablespoons garlic salt
> 2 tablespoons sesame seeds
> Pinch cayenne pepper
> 1 cup mayonnaise (preferably homemade)
> 1 cup buttermilk
> 2 tablespoons lemon juice

Combine the dry ingredients in a bowl, and set aside. Whisk the remaining ingredients together and add ¼ cup of the dry mixture. Stir until well blended. May be used at once, though flavor improves when dressing is allowed to set in the refrigerator for an hour or more. The dried mixture keeps indefinitely in a sealed container. The dressing will keep for a week in the refrigerator. Makes 2 cups of dressing for every ¼ cup of dry mix.

Good Reading

- Valerie Flournoy. *The Patchwork Quilt.* N.Y.: Dial Books for Young Readers, 1985. (Ages 6 to 10)
- Eve Rice. *At Grammy's House.* N.Y.: Greenwillow Books, 1990. (Ages 4 to 8)

Just Us

Simple Fun

Look through family albums together. Explain to children who everyone is so they have a sense of family. Discuss which state each relative lives in (refer to an atlas if necessary), what job each one holds, how old each is, and how each one of them is related to your children.

Here are two "grandparent and child"–tested pastimes that are loved by both generations.

Squiggles   (Ages 4 and Up)

Place a "squiggle" on a 3- by 5-inch or 5- by 7-inch piece of paper. (A Squiggle is a drawing of a simple shape, such as an "S," and "X," a lightning bolt, or a geometric shape—something basic that can be left up to the interpretation of each person.) Provide all players with the same squiggles. The object of the game is to see how each person can take the same basic shape and turn it into a unique drawing of his own!

Thumb Prints   (Ages 3 and Up)

This is the same idea as the previous game, except that each person uses her own thumb to make a "thumb print" on a piece of paper. Players can then turn their thumb prints into all sorts of imaginative works of art—mice, cats, faces, etc. Provide ink pads (with washable ink) and pads of paper. Try using different colored ink pads for interest.

Through the Years

Many older people have no grandchildren to call their own. Some have no family or nearby relatives, and live lives of quiet isolation. September 12 is a good day to let kids know that they can make a difference in someone's life. Check your neighborhood, church, or synagogue for any older people living alone who might enjoy a visit. Nursing homes often allow small groups of older children to visit patients on a one-on-one basis for a short period of time.

There are many things children can do to honor a "grandparent":

- Surprise an elderly neighbor with a small gift of baked goods, a poem, or a drawing

• Ask an older person what his own childhood was like. Where did he live? What was school like? What job did he have?

• Get to know someone's likes and dislikes—what's her favorite color? song? hobby? food to eat? movie? If the kids aren't familiar with the answer—investigate. Plan a trip to the library to learn more. Find someone who has an album or tape with the song and listen to it. Ask kids what they think of the song or movie.

School Days

With the onset of autumn comes the end of vacation and the return to school. With the next two projects kids can personalize their textbooks and learn how to make homemade paper—great for a special project and a real teacher-pleaser!

PAPER CAPERS

Cool Cover-Ups   (AGES 5 AND UP, WITH HELP)

Who wants to lug around plain old textbooks? Not most kids. Instead, help them create some personalized covers. Start with a basic paper cover—a recycled brown paper bag is the most commonly used cover, though any sturdy paper will do. Try shelf paper or shiny wrapping paper in plain white or a favorite color.

Measure the height and width (both sides, plus the spine) of the book and cut the paper to fit, leaving an extra 6 inches in the width to allow for a 3-inch flap for the inside of the front and back covers. There are many ways children can personalize their covers. Check the index (page 249) for paper crafts, or try the following marbling technique.

Marbling Paper   (AGES 7 AND UP)

Marbling is a fun technique to use on book folders. Since it requires the use of oil paints and paint thinner, it is best done under adult supervision.

Assorted oil paints in favorite colors
Paper cups
Paint thinner
A large, shallow pan
Water
Unflavored gelatin
A wide-tooth comb, with several teeth missing
Plain paper book cover
A stack of newspaper

Place a tablespoon or two of oil paint in a paper cup. Add a few tea-spoons of paint thinner and stir to blend. Continue thinning individual colors until the paints are the consistency of tempera paints. Place about an inch of water in the pan and stir in the gelatin until well blended. Place a few drops of paint on the water. The paint will float on top of the water. (As children will be using pans of varying sizes, and different brands of paints, etc., there is no one correct proportion of ingredients. Experiment with the water-to-gelatin ratio and paint-to-thinner ratio until the paint floats on the surface.) Start with one color or add several according to the desired effect. To achieve the marbling effect, swirl the comb through the water in varying directions. Carefully lower the book cover on to the top of the water. Tap lightly with your finger to release any trapped air bubbles. Gently lift the paper up, turn it over quickly, and lay it on top of several layers of newspaper. Allow to dry.

Making Paper   (AGES 5 AND UP, WITH HELP)

Children will enjoy making paper to use in various school projects. Homemade paper also makes wonderful writing paper, greeting cards, or leaves in the following bookmaking projects. The art of paper making dates back to A.D. 105, when a Chinese man named Ts'ai Lun developed the process. Though nearly all paper now is made from wood pulp, almost any fibrous material will work. The easiest method involves recycling old paper—paper towels, computer paper, newspaper, junk mail, old greeting cards.

4 ¾-inch-square pieces of wood, two 8 inches long and two 10½ inches long
Hammer and 1-inch nails

City Watch

Many kids who live in the city have an "urban advantage." Within a matter of miles are many of the nation's best museums and cultural resources. Take advantage of the opportunity! Make it a point to visit local attractions at least once a month.

An 8- by 10½-inch piece of window screening
Assorted types of paper
Blender
A pan or tub (larger than 8 by 10½ inches)
A dry sponge
Paper towels

Simple Fun

Add stickers or small toys to kids' lunchboxes for extra fun at lunchtime. Write kids quick messages when packing their lunch—"I Love You" or "You're Doing Great" go a long way toward making kids feel proud and secure.

Hammer the four pieces of wood together to make a rectangular frame (called the "mold"). Fit the screening over the mold and nail down all around on one side. Tear the assorted pieces of paper into small pieces. Fill the blender ¾ full of water, add the paper pieces, and puree into a pulp (called the "slurry"). Pour 2 to 3 blender-fulls of the slurry into the pan. Hold the frame with the screen side up and slide it into the slurry. Make sure the slurry is evenly distributed over the screen before slowly lifting it out and letting the excess water drain back into the pan. Carefully invert the screen onto several layers of paper towels and blot the back with a sponge to absorb any excess water. Carefully hold on to one corner of the frame and lift up the screen. The slurry (now called "wet-leaf") will remain on the paper toweling. Place a piece of paper towel on the top and iron dry. Gently turn the "wet-leaf," leaving the paper towel in place, place another piece of paper towel on top and iron dry. Remove paper toweling—voilà! A sheet of homemade paper!

Note: *Children can achieve different interesting effects by combining paper and other fibrous materials to make the slurry. Try adding grass, flowers, leaves, weeds, bark, celery strings, carrots, or beets. Chop up and add to a blender container that is ¾ full of water. Puree, add to paper-water slurry, and stir to blend. (As adults may frown on putting the family blender to experimental use, check out local yard sales and junk shops for secondhand blenders!)*

A Handmade Booklet (AGES 5 AND UP)

Often, certain creative writing projects in school can be taken one step further by being presented in a handmade booklet. Children should check with their teachers first to make sure that this is agreeable. Booklets make wonderful gifts and become cherished keepsakes when filled with a child's own thoughts, poems, or drawings.

> *A book cover*
> *2 endpapers*
> *3 or more heavy pieces of paper (paper should be slightly smaller than the cover when folded in half)*
> *Yarn*
> *Scissors*
> *Glue*

Set the book cover and end papers aside. Fold the pieces of paper in half and stack them one inside the next. Using a hole puncher, punch holes ½ inch from the fold, spacing them about ½ inch apart. Lace the yarn in and out of the holes. Secure ends by knotting.

THE GREAT FOOD DEBATE

During the school year getting children to eat right can be one of the biggest battles of raising a family. Mornings are a rush as families get ready for work, school, and daily household chores. Breakfasts are often eaten standing up or left half-finished as everyone races to beat the clock! Lunches can remain a mystery as parents

Good Reading

- Gloria Houston. *My Great-Aunt Arizona.* N.Y.: HarperCollins, 1992. (Ages 5 to 9)
- Marilyn Burns. *The I Hate Mathematics! Book* and *Math for Smarty Pants.* CA: Brown Paper Books, 1975 and 1982. (Ages 9 to 14)

KID-SOURCE

Science-By-Mail
Museum of Science
Science Park
Boston, MA 02114-1099
800-729-3300
A science education program for children in grades 4 to 9 that pairs kids with volunteer scientists.

Odyssey
Cobblestone Publishing, Inc.
7 School Street
Peterborough, NH 03458
800-821-0115
Science magazine for kids ages 8 to 14. One-year subscription $22.95.

send kids to school with lunch boxes packed with nutritious offerings—only to find out that their "good intentions" were swapped for little Zach's lunch of bologna sandwich, soda, and a brownie! After-school snacks are often convenience foods, while dinners can become a time of enormous frustration as finicky children pepper their dinner conversation with "What's that?", "Yuck," or "Gross!"

Here are some family-tested ideas and recipes, starting with breakfast, that will win raves from your crowd.

Start Your A.M. Engines!

Breakfast is an important time (though hurried!) in our house. I drive our daughter to her school, which is an hour away, and we leave the house at seven. It's important that the first meal of the day be nutritious and tasty so those "little engines" can carry through to lunchtime. Here are some of our favorite breakfast ideas:

- Cereals are quick, easy, and a good source of fiber. Try to choose whole-grain products without artificial ingredients or added sweeteners. Our favorites include: Barbara's Multigrain Shredded Spoonfuls, Erewhon's Instant Oatmeal, Cheerios, and Shredded Wheat. Hot cereals can be made the night before, refrigerated, and warmed on the stove or in the microwave while everyone's getting ready. Though we occasionally serve them with milk, I try to offer them with juice, soy milk, or a vanilla-almond beverage available in natural food stores. Topped with a bit of maple syrup or brown rice syrup, cereals are a bit more nutritious than when sprinkled with sugar. Serve plain or with fruit.
- Pancakes and waffles can be made up once a week in a large batch and then frozen in serving sizes in resealable plastic bags. Served with maple syrup, apple butter, jam or yogurt, and fresh fruit, they're especially nutritious when made with whole-grain flours.
- Muffins are a favorite of children, especially when baked in the mini-muffin tins. Full of complex carbohydrates (energy food!), they can be a good way of adding additional vegetables and fruits to a child's diet. Try them with grated carrot, zucchini, or apple, or with banana, strawberry, blueberry, or cranberry. Can be served plain or with fruit butter instead of butter.

- Apple Cake is a favorite breakfast treat. Look for the recipe on page 205.
- Morning orange or apple juice with ¼ cup fresh carrot juice added packs extra nutrition!

S C H O O L L U N C H E S

Here's one of my favorite recipes for a lunch box. As a real time saver I usually double the recipe when we have it for dinner, so there's plenty left over for a quick and easy sandwich for school the next day.

The Best Turkey Meatloaf

This Turkey Meatloaf is a healthy twist on the traditional version made with red meats. Served in a pita pocket with shredded lettuce and some grated carrots, it's a great lunch-box addition. Anyone who has ever tried this has asked for the recipe.

2 pounds ground turkey
⅔ cup minced onion
⅓ cup minced celery
1 tablespoon minced garlic
1 tablespoon grated carrot
1 tablespoon canola oil
2 eggs
½ cup fine dry bread crumbs
½ cup cooked kashi (available in gourmet or health food markets)
½ cup minced parsley
1 teaspoon Dijon mustard
¼ teaspoon seasoned salt (Herbamare or Crazy Jane's salt are good choices)

Preheat the oven to 350°F. Place ground turkey in a medium-size bowl and set aside. Sauté the onion, celery, garlic, and carrot in the oil until soft. Add to the turkey along with the remaining ingredients and combine well. Shape into a loaf and place in a pan. Bake about 45 to 55 minutes, or until no longer pink. Pour off the pan juices to use in the sauce.

Sauce

Measure pan juices and add milk to make ½ cup liquid. Pour a few tablespoons into a small saucepan and sprinkle in 2 teaspoons flour. Stir till well blended. Pour in remaining liquid and bring to a boil. Reduce the heat and cook for 3 or 4 minutes until thickened. Remove from the heat and whisk in 1 teaspoon mustard (optional). Serve over Turkey Meatloaf. Sprinkle with additional minced parsley if desired.

Halloween

It's no wonder children look forward to this holiday! Halloween gives kids a chance to dress up in costumes, collect (and usually eat!) way too much candy, scare the dickens out of themselves or others, and have a rollicking good time!

Many adults today want to keep their goblins and ghosts close to home and monitor the goodies that go into the treat bags. More and more children are going to Halloween parties, either at home or at school instead of going on the traditional door-to-door "trick or treat." With spooky music, a costume contest (funniest, scariest, most original), goodie bags full of cool stuff, and the following fun things to do, kids will especially look forward to having a Halloween party every year!

The Ghost Tree   (AGES 5 AND UP)

No Halloween table is complete without a tree covered with little white ghosts. Great as a centerpiece, the branches can be saved and used for other seasonal parties. (See Easter Egg Tree, Thankful Tree, and Resolution Tree.)

Find a bushy branch or two with no leaves. Fill a clay pot with dampened, dried flower Oasis and secure the stems in it. Cover the top of the Oasis with woodland moss or purchased Spanish moss. Make the ghosts and hang them on the tree. Look for a small owl or cat in area novelty shops, and place in the crook of the branches. Break a wooden tongue-depressor or plant marker in half and write R.I.P. (Rest In Peace) across the top. Poke into the moss, for an eerie graveyard!

Simple Fun

Make spooky "ghosts." Fold a piece of black construction paper in half the long way. Unfold and pour 1 teaspoon white acrylic paint into the crease. Let children press along fold. Unfold and lay flat to dry. Add black eyes and mouth with a black felt tip pen if desired.

Ghosts

(Ages 5 and Up)

White cotton fabric
Cotton balls, wool, or fiberfill
White thread
Orange yarn
Black felt-tip pen

Cut the cotton fabric into 5-inch squares. Place a cotton ball in the center of each square. Gather fabric around the ball to form the "head," and tie with a piece of thread. Make sure the thread is long enough to tie into a loop so the ghost can hang from a branch. Tie a length of orange yarn around neck, knot it, and snip ends. Draw eyes on the head with a felt marker. Hang ghosts all over the branches.

Spiderweb Placemats

(Ages 4 and Up, with Help)

These are easy for kids to make and look great with "ghost" napkins:

Black construction paper
White paint
Jelly roll pan with a 1-inch lip
A marble

Cut black construction paper into a circle that will fit inside the pan. (A plate makes a great circular pattern for a spiderweb.) Place the paper circle inside the pan and place 1 teaspoon white paint in the middle of the circle. Drop the marble into the pan, and with a back and forth motion, tilt the pan so that the marble rolls through the paint and makes a spider web pattern.

Ghost Napkin

(Ages 5 and Up)

Use a few pieces of foil- or cellophane-wrapped candy for the "head." Place in the center of a white dinner napkin, and tie with a length of orange yarn to form the neck. Draw on eyes with a black marker.

Simple Fun

Make Monster Mitts from clear plastic gloves! Stuff one glove inside another—double-bag style—and stuff the fingertips with candy corn. Fill the rest of the glove with caramel-coated popcorn. Secure the end with rubber bands and holiday colored ribbons. Put a plastic "spider" ring on each glove!

Chestnut Cobwebs   (AGES 6 AND UP, WITH HELP)

We make these in the autumn, when chestnuts are plentiful. They make a great party activity and look wonderful when hung from the ceiling with dental floss!

A big chestnut
Awl or large needle
Eight toothpicks
White, black, or colored floss

Using the awl or needle, make eight ¼-inch holes in a circle around the middle of the chestnut. Secure a toothpick in each of the holes with a dab of glue. Tie one end of a very long piece of floss to one of the toothpicks. Push knot down toothpick so it's close to the chestnut. Wrap floss around the next toothpick and continue wrapping each successive toothpick, leaving a space each time you go around to resemble a real spider's web. (Alternatively, you can push strands close together for a solid weave.) When a knot is necessary, try to make it a small one, and have it on the back side, out of sight. Stop weaving about ¼ inch from the ends of the toothpicks. Knot the floss several times on the last toothpick. Leave enough floss so the cobweb can be hung. About 12 inches is good.

Halloween Nonsense   (AGES 5 AND UP)

Have children practice these during the weeks before Halloween!

Spook-tacular Tongue Twisters

Which witch wished the wicked wish?
Seven skeletons shrieked shrill, scary songs.

Rib Ticklers

Q: How do witches play baseball?
A: With their bats.

Q: What do goblins eat for dessert?
A: Scream puffs.

Simple Fun

Carving pumpkins takes a bit of skill and is time-consuming. Let kids decorate their pumpkins with black felt-tip markers! Draw on spooky faces—add red and white paint for eyes and mouth!

Q: What does the witch's broom do when it is tired?
A: It goes to sweep.

Q: What gum do ghosts like the best?
A: Boo-ble gum.

Q: Why didn't the ghost stay locked in his room?
A: He was just passing through.

Magic Broomstick Brew

Have you ever wondered what was stirring in those giant black kettles? Well, here's a brew that will chase away the cold! They say *this* is what makes those broomsticks fly! Float an apple studded with cloves in the punch for a festive touch.

> 4 cups water
> 8 cinnamon-apple herbal tea bags
> 2 tablespoons honey
> 2 cups apple juice
> 2 cups cherry juice (try Very Cherry by After the Fall—available in
>   health food stores and in many major grocery stores)

Bring the water to a boil. Remove from heat; add tea bags and allow to steep for 5 minutes. Discard tea bags and stir in remaining ingredients. Serve at once or keep warm at a low simmer. Makes 8 cups.

Black Cats

No Halloween party is complete without these little kitties! Make an extra batch or two so guests can take home a few in their trick-or-treat bags.

> 3¼ cups unbleached flour
> ¾ cup unsweetened cocoa powder
> ¼ teaspoon salt
> 2 sticks unsalted butter
> 1⅔ cups sugar
> 2 eggs
> 1 teaspoon vanilla

Combine the flour, cocoa, and salt in a medium-size bowl and stir to blend. Cream the butter and sugar in the bowl of a mixer until light and fluffy. Add the eggs one at a time, scraping the bowl after each addition. Add flour mixture and beat on low until well blended. Turn out onto waxed paper, pat into a ball, and chill, covered, for several hours or overnight.

Preheat the oven to 350°F. Lightly flour a flat surface and roll the dough out to ¼-inch thickness. Cut with "cat" cookie cutters or assorted Halloween shapes. Line two baking sheets with foil and bake for about 8 to 10 minutes. Do not allow cookies to brown. Makes about 5 dozen cookies.

GAMES TO PLAY

Crazy Mixed-Up Webs! (AGES 4 AND UP)

This is a great activity to start off a Halloween party! Have a different color yarn for each child. Begin with one color, and tie it to an object, such as a chair leg. Unwind the yarn as you wrap it once around various other things in the room—a table leg, drawer knob, etc. Have the yarn go from one side of the room to the other,

avoiding anything too high for kids to manage. Once the first color has been unwound and secured, go on to the next color, until there is one color of yarn wound around the room for each child. On the word "Go," let each child unwind the yarn, rolling it into a ball as he or she progresses. The first child to get his yarn all into a ball wins, or for a noncompetitive version, give a favor to each child as she finishes unwinding.

Children today will delight in these two old-time frivolities from long ago.

Maritime Fortunes   (AGES 4 AND UP)

Children will need walnut shell boats and a large basin of water for this fortune-telling activity. To make a walnut shell boat: Glue a small piece of paper to a toothpick for a sail. Place a piece of play-dough or clay inside an empty walnut shell half, and secure the sail. Have each child identify her vessel by writing her name on the sail. Each child can set her boat adrift on the "sea of life," represented by the water. Have one person make waves by tilting the tub slightly or roughing up the water with a stick. Several predictions can be made based on the actions of the boats:

- Two boats that come in contact with each other: the two respective owners will engage in mutual interests together—perhaps a business or a hobby.
- One boat sails in front of another: likewise, these two people will cross each other's path in life.
- Two boats sail close to each other and continue along the same course: the owners will spend their lives in the same way.
- A boat stays close to the side of the tub, rather than sailing out into the open water: the person will stick close to home, instead of venturing off into the world.

The Mysterious Moonlight   (AGES 5 AND UP)

How deliciously eerie the full moon seems on Halloween night! Those wishing to divine its powers may put it to special use on this holiday eve. Have a child hold a handheld mirror and venture forth to an open door or window. To determine how many bright prospects there are for the coming year, have the child hold up the mirror so that it catches the reflection of the moon, while keeping his reflection inside the mirror. However many moons are seen, reflected in the mirror, represent how often good fortune will come to him before the next Halloween!

SECRET CODES

Elementary school children love speaking in their own secret language! Certainly every school across America (as well as around the world) has special messages being passed back and forth—tucked in the low branches of a favored schoolyard tree, in the chinks of an old wall, or passed between hands. Let's look at some of these secret languages children use to communicate with each other.

Pig Latin   (AGES 7 AND UP)

This is usually the first "pretend" language that school-age children learn. I remember being in awe of the kids in my class who could rattle off whole sentences at breakneck speed! It's really pretty easy to learn, as there are only three steadfast rules:

- Rule Number One. For a word beginning with a vowel (*a, e, i, o, u*), add "way" to the end of the word. Example: *are*, are-way; *ever*, ever-way; *in*, in-way.
- Rule Number Two. For a word beginning with a single consonant, move the consonant to the end of the word, and add "ay." Example: *move*, ove-may; *locker*, ocker-lay; *today*, oday-tay.
- Rule Number Three. For a word beginning with two or more consonants (*th, ch, sh, thr*), move the group of consonants to the end of the word, and add "ay." Example: *three*, ee-threay; *children*, ildren-chay; *please*, ease-play.

Computer Codes   (AGES 7 AND UP)

Kids can develop their own languages by using their computers or typewriters. First type the letters of the alphabet in a continuous

Simple Fun

Use Invisible Ink for that special message! All children need is lemon juice and a small paintbrush. Dip the brush in the juice and write on white paper. Dry thoroughly. To read: Turn on a lamp and place the paper up close to the light—the heat will make the words magically appear!

line, leaving a space between each letter. Above each individual letter type a "secret symbol." Children should make a few copies of their code—since the symbols are haphazardly chosen, kids probably won't remember the symbols without a master plan to refer to! Here's an example:

2 ~ $ 8 & □ ↓ " : % ; @ ^ (_) = \ [/ 7 , 5 + !
A B C D E F G H I J K L M N O P Q R S T U V W X Y Z

~#^ + (/ =8#$ [↓"\ ¿ (Translation: Can you read this¿)

As an alternative try a variation of the computer code using all numbers instead of keyboard symbols. The easiest one to start out with has A = 1, B = 2, and so on until you reach Z = 26. Let kids start out with this one, and once they get the hang of it, they can go on to one a bit more complicated where the numbers are out of order, such as Random Start. This variation has A = whatever number the children choose to start with, say 10. B would = 11, C = 12, D = 13, and so on until Z = 35.

The Greek Spiral Code (AGES 7 AND UP)

Here's a method of writing a secret message first developed by Greek soldiers as they waged battle against their enemies. All you need to begin is a length of paper about 44 inches long (3 feet, 8 inches), a cardboard tube that's left over from inside a roll of paper towels, two rubber bands, and a pen. Use four sheets of paper towels (don't tear them apart, you want a continuous length of paper to wrap around your tube); cut a ½-inch strip—the long way—the entire length of the paper towels. Children can also use lengths of newspaper, wrapping paper, etc.

Wrap one end of the paper strip around one end of the tube and secure with a rubber band. Continue to wrap the paper strip around the tube so the edges are close to each other but don't overlap. Once you have finished wrapping the paper around the tube secure the other end with the additional rubber band. Now you are ready to write your secret message!! Start anywhere on the tube and write as you normally would, from left to right, being careful to put only one letter on each section of paper, and leaving a space (one section) between words. Once the message is finished, carefully remove the strip from the tube, fold it up carefully and deliver it to your friend. Make sure to tell each other what kind of tube was used, as the size will determine whether or not the other person will be able to read the message! Other cylinders that work well are pencils, pens, markers, frozen juice cans, and flashlights.

Tic-Tac-Toe Code   (AGES 7 AND UP)

All kids of a certain age know how to play tic-tac-toe. Not many know that it can also serve as the basis for a "private message"! Draw three tic-tac-toe frames and put the letters of the alphabet into the squares. Start with "A" in the upper left-hand corner of the first frame, "B" in the middle frame, and "C" in the upper right-hand frame. Continue placing letters until you come to "Z." ("J" will start the second frame, and "R" will end it. "S" will start the third frame, and "Z" will be the last letter, with one blank space left.) Place one dot under each letter from "J" through "R."

Place two dots under each letter from "S" through "Z." Each letter will be represented by the lines around it, and the absence or inclusion of one or two dots. Example:

Meet me at two.

Note: *If kids want a really secret code, have them alter the sequence of letters within the frames. As an example, have the letters go up and down instead of sideways or start with "Z" as the first letter, etc. They'll have a code no one can crack!!*

Flash!

The ability of mariners and explorers to use the sun to send signals is legendary. Children, especially if they're neighbors, can communicate with each other by transmitting a series of flashes simply by using a mirror and a piece of cardboard that is larger than the mirror. Determine a code before: two flashes, three flashes, etc. There should be a 3- to 4-second pause between each flash, and at least a 20- to 30-second pause between messages. Some suggestions for messages:

- Come right over
- Don't come over
- Call me on the phone
- Meet me at the . . . (have a prearranged location) in 15 minutes
- Let's do something fun! (movies, playground, skateboard, rollerblading, etc.)

On a sunny day, a child can send a message to a friend sitting about thirty feet away by sitting and facing the sun or positioning herself so the sun is overhead. She can then try to capture the sunlight on her mirror. Kids should practice reflecting the light on the ground or at particular objects. Now the child can tilt the mirror so that the light aims at the friend. (Have the friend wave when she sees the light from the mirror.) Hold the mirror steady—bracing it against one's body will help. Using the piece of cardboard, the child covers and then uncovers the mirror to send the signal. Every time the mirror is covered and then uncovered counts as one flash.

Note: *Children can use a variation of the mirror method and send signals at night by using a flashlight. We've done this when the kids were playing in an outdoor tent in the yard after dark. My husband was in the tent with them while I was in the house. Some of the messages we used were: "We're thirsty," "We're hungry," "Bring more bug spray," "We're A-OK." (Mine to them was "5 minutes before you have to come in"!)*

BITS OF NONSENSE

Recess is a time when kids get together to trade jokes, silly sayings, secret messages, and other such rites of passage through childhood. I'm always amazed when my daughter brings home a joke or a bit of nonsense and I tell her "I remember that from when I was a little girl!"

Do you carrot all for me?

My heart beets for you,
With your turnip nose
And your radish face
You are a peach.
If we cantaloupe,
Lettuce marry;
Weed make a swell pear.

Mississippi said to Missouri,
"If I put on my New Jersey
What will Delaware?"
Virginia said, "Alaska."

I'm rubber and you're glue.
What you say to me
Will bounce back,
and stick to you.

Through the teeth,
Past the gums,
Look out, stomach,
Here it comes!

A peanut sat on the railroad track,
His heart was all a-flutter!
Along came a train,
Toot, Toot! Peanut Butter!

Ladies and jelly spoons:
I come before you
To stand behind you
And tell you something
I know nothing about!

Silly Sign-Offs   (AGES 5 AND UP)

Letter writing seems almost to be a thing of the past. Children can
be encouraged to write when provided with colorful paper, brightly
colored pens, and an assortment of interesting stamps. Here's a few
"bons mots" to get kids going!

UR
2 good
2 Be
4 got 10.

Can't think,
Brain numb.
Inspiration
Won't come.
Poor ink,
Bad pen.
That's all.
Amen.

I've thought and thought and thought in vain;
At last I think I'll sign my name.

Some write for pleasure,
Some write for fame,
But I write only
To sign my name.

The Last Word

Till the mail boxes!
Till the skate boards!

Till the chocolate chips!
Till the soda pops!
Till the kitchen sinks!

Betcha Can't Say This!

Toy boat, toy boat, toy boat!

She sells sea shells by the sea shore.

A skunk sat on a stump. The stump thunk the skunk stunk.
The skunk thunk the stump stunk.

How much wood could a woodchuck chuck
If a woodchuck could chuck wood?
He would chuck what wood a woodchuck could chuck,
If a woodchuck could chuck wood.

If Peter Piper picked a peck of pickled peppers,
a peck of pickled peppers Peter Piper picked.
But if Peter Piper picked a peck of pickled peppers,
where is the peck of pickled peppers Peter Piper picked?

Thanksgiving

It was right before Thanksgiving several years ago, when we were living in our log cabin on eastern Long Island, that I first started taking notes for this book. The air was cool and crisp during those weeks before Thanksgiving—with winter just a breath away! The house was full of delightful smells from the various foods we were cooking in the antique woodstove. Our big farm table was covered with pinecones, nuts, berry branches, and leaves—treasures the children and I had found in the woods behind the house and brought home for our centerpiece. Thanksgiving has always been my favorite family holiday, and a time to treasure those whom we hold dear to our hearts.

GIVING THANKS

When guests come to our home for Thanksgiving they usually stay overnight. This was true when we spent Thanksgiving in New York, and even more so now that we live in Florida! For this reason family activities, games, and pastimes have always been a big part of our holiday and a sure way to entertain a large group of varying ages:

- Several days before Thanksgiving we check with the local shelters about baking an extra turkey, some side dishes, and a few desserts. The children think of this as caring for our "extended family" and join in happily with grocery shopping, unloading the car, and cooking. It's with great pride and satisfaction that they announce "I made that" or "I helped with this!"

Simple Fun

Let children cut ½-inch slices of sweet potato into holiday shapes with tiny cookie cutters! Great for decorating side dishes such as mashed potatoes or pureed squash.

Simple Fun

Play "Pass the Apple." Form a line with three or more people. The first player places an apple under his chin, with hands behind his back, and passes the apple to the second player, who must take it under her chin and pass it on to the next person, and so on. Form teams for another version. The first team to pass the apple to the end of the line wins!

• After the meal is a great time to work on the family photo album. Have a few new albums on hand and let the children help sort and place photographs in the pages. It's a great way to remember and reminisce as a family; and to reflect on the passing year and all that you have to be thankful for.

• Let the children help with setting the table. There are napkins to fold, small pieces of silver to polish (this was a favorite activity at my daughter's school), and dishes and silverware to place. Don't forget to set a place for someone not able to join you. One season my mother was not able to join us from her home on Cape Cod and the children took great care in lovingly setting her place. Later, they mailed the placecard, some photographs, and other holiday mementos to her.

• Make "Thank You for Being You" placecards. One year we wanted to do something different for our placecards so the children and I cut out old photographs of each person who would be joining us for Thanksgiving dinner and illustrated it by drawing little pictures showing each person's favorite hobbies and interests. We sent one to Nana the year she couldn't join us, decorated with crossword puzzles, flowers, letter tiles from a Scrabble game, and a message from the children.

• Start a "Holidays" book. We started one at Thanksgiving one year and had added to it during all major celebrations since. In it we have listed each holiday's date, the guests, the menu, and a description of our decorations. Usually guests bring a special home-cooked dish or pie. When one receives special accolades I make sure to include the recipe in our holidays book!

• Children will love making bread dough napkin rings (see page 53 for dough recipe) for the Thanksgiving table. Make a ring of dough, and flatten one side of it so it stands up on the cookie sheet. Crumple up a piece of tinfoil and place it inside the ring to keep it from collapsing while cooking. Follow directions for cooking. Rings can be decorated with small pieces of dough cut out of various shapes—the person's initials or the first letter of her name, small overlapping leaves, or a miniature turkey. Small cookie cutters work well for this. Painted in fall colors with non-toxic water-base paints, they are a constant reminder all year long of a lovely holiday celebration.

• Take advantage of having various generations together under the same roof and put together a Family Tree. You'll need a large piece of construction paper. Let the children start with themselves and work their way backward through the generations: add parents, grandparents, great-grandparents and any step-parents, aunts, uncles, and relatives of their choice. Children may choose to add photographs (an Instamatic camera is great for this!) and vital facts about each person.

• I was about to pack away our Ghost Tree one year when I thought of a way to extend it into our Thanksgiving celebration. I packed away the "ghosts" and moved the branches to our coffee table in front of the fireplace. The children and I placed a leaf that they had cut out of colored construction paper at each place setting. On the back we wrote each person's name. At the end of the meal I explained that the children would like for each person to write down what they were most thankful for. The children then gathered all the leaves and hung them on the branches of our Thankful Tree. After dessert we moved to the living room and let each person take a turn reading a leaf. The variety of answers from the children (and adults!) was enlightening—from "I am thankful for the sun" to

Simple Fun

Make festive Indians and Pilgrims for the holiday table. Stuff a small brown bag with paper, fold down the top, and glue in place. Cut a face, hair, arms, and two feet from construction paper and glue them in place. Draw on clothing and decorate with crayons and markers. Add a hat and feathers.

"I am thankful for my dog" and "I am thankful for having enough to eat."

Holiday Bingo (AGES 5 AND UP)

This game can be adapted to any holiday. Have kids help think of 15 words associated with Thanksgiving, such as: Thanksgiving, turkey, Indian, Pilgrim, squash, pumpkin, corn, pie, cranberries, walnuts, pecans, orange, yellow, red, and black. Each player is given a sheet of paper which is divided into 9 squares (older children and adults may prefer playing with a card divided into 15 squares). The center square is labeled "free," and the remaining squares each have one word from the list. Be sure to mix up the order in which the words are written for each card. Have someone call out the words one at a time. The winner is the one who gets three consecutive squares in a row.

Simple Fun

Make "Handprint Turkeys." Each child traces her hand on construction paper (splay fingers out for the best effect). Draw the head on the thumb, and the legs at the base of the palm. Decorate with crayons, markers, paint, or by gluing on bits of colored paper.

THE HOLIDAY FEAST

Eating is serious business on Thanksgiving! Have you ever stopped to picture in your mind all those tables across America, full of turkey, stuffing, cranberry relish, candied yams, and other traditional fare? This holiday is usually not the time to try out a new dish without giving the family fair warning—my husband was horrified one year when I decided to try stuffed onions instead of his favorite creamed ones!

Our daughter Lauren always requests Popovers—"that bread that puffs up"—and little Hunter sits contentedly each Thanksgiving dipping apple slices into his beloved fondue!

Cheese Fondue

We always have a chafing dish full of fondue at Thanksgiving. Our family gathers early in the day for outdoor walks to the pond, joint wood-chopping sessions, and games with the kids. Often this is all we'll eat until our big holiday meal. Cheese Fondue is a great way to take advantage of autumn's bounty—dip chunks of McIntosh apples, steamed brussels sprouts, cauliflower, broccoli, and toasted pieces of French bread into the warm sauce.

3 tablespoons unsalted butter
3 tablespoons flour
1 teaspoon dry mustard
1½ cups beer* or chicken broth
1 pound cheddar cheese, grated
½ teaspoon horseradish
Dash of Tabasco
Freshly grated pepper

Melt the butter in a small pan, over low heat. Whisk in the flour and the dry mustard and cook for 5 minutes, stirring constantly. Whisk in the beer or chicken broth and stir for an additional 10 minutes, until thick. Melt the cheese in a medium-size pan, over the lowest setting. Add the flour mixture and the remaining ingredients to the melted cheese and stir until thick and well blended. Can be kept warm in a covered chafing dish over low heat, or may be made ahead, refrigerated, and warmed gently over a pan of simmering water when needed. Set out the goodies to be dipped in the fondue, and give everyone a fondue fork.

*You may substitute chicken broth for the beer, though the taste will be milder. The alcohol in the beer dissipates with the cooking and poses no threat to children.

Gingerbread

This gingerbread is a much lighter version than the traditional recipe. We serve this for dessert in addition to pumpkin pie. It's wonderful warm from the oven with a dollop of freshly whipped cinnamon whipped cream on top! A real favorite with children.

2 cups unbleached flour
2 teaspoons baking powder
1 teaspoon baking soda
¼ teaspoon salt
1½ teaspoons powdered ginger

1 teaspoon cinnamon
Dash of nutmeg
¼ teaspoon orange zest
4 tablespoons (¼ cup) unsalted butter
½ cup light brown sugar, firmly packed
2 eggs
1 cup sour cream
¼ cup dark molasses

Preheat the oven to 350°F. and place a rack in the middle of the oven. Butter a 6- by 8-inch glass baking dish and set aside. In a large bowl measure the flour, baking powder, baking soda, salt, ginger, cinnamon, nutmeg, and orange zest. Set aside. Cream the butter and brown sugar in the bowl of an electric mixer. Add the eggs and beat until light and fluffy. Add the sour cream and molasses. Gradually add the dry ingredients to the mixture. Beat well, being sure to scrape down the sides of the bowl after each addition. Bake in the prepared pan for 45 to 50 minutes, or until a toothpick inserted in the middle comes out clean. Cool gingerbread in the pan for 5 minutes before cutting into serving pieces. Yields 12 2-inch squares.

For topping: Whip ½ pint of heavy cream with ½ teaspoon of sugar and a dash of cinnamon. Serve the gingerbread warm, with a spoonful of whipped cream on top.

Young Hearts and Hands

By learning about other lands and different cultures, families can plant the seeds of respect and understanding in their children.

Getting to Know Another Country (or State)
(AGES 3 TO ADULT)

To get started all you need is a world map or globe. Let children take turns closing their eyes and pointing to a country. Once the location has been chosen, do all you can to learn as much as you can for one week. Some suggestions include:

• Taking a family trip to the library and searching for information on your adopted country. Geographical books for kids and travel guides are helpful. Ask the librarian for suggestions on any good fairy tales or children's literature pertaining to your location.
• Hang up a travel poster from a local travel agency to help your family get in the mood.
• Choose some favorite foods from your country and try them out. This could include ordering take-out food or visiting local ethnic markets and trying out a recipe of two. Store clerks are often helpful in suggesting easy and tasty dishes.
• Have a family discussion about your chosen country. What is the climate like? Is it similar or different from yours? What do the people wear? What holidays do they celebrate?
• Listen to music from your country. Music for Little People (800-727-2233) and many local libraries stock a selection of music from around the world.

Simple Fun

Encourage kids to read about children from other cultures. Check the multicultural section at your local library for some popular titles.

- Learn some simple greetings. Is anyone in your school from the country you have chosen? Ask them what they like most about their country. What do they like the least?

How many families are familiar with all fifty American states? Not many, I'm sure! Get to know your states by pointing to a location on a map of the United States or by drawing straws. See if older children and adults can name all the states (this can be a game itself!).

Enthusiasm Is Infectious! (Ages 6 and Up)

Many children believe that they as one person cannot make a difference. It's true that preschoolers can't do much about diminishing rain forests, disappearing wetlands, and unbalanced ecosystems, though older kids and teenagers can make an impact. First kids have to determine what they think is important—maybe they want to start a group of beach clean-up volunteers, help find homes for abandoned cats in their neighborhood, set up a juice box recycling program in their school, or bring unwanted toys and books from neighbors and friends to kids living in local shelters. Wherever their interest lies, it's important for us as adults to let them know they *can* make a difference. Children are born with a natural wonder, love, and compassion for their fellow creatures that inhabit the earth. When these traits are fostered and nurtured in children they will influence their thoughts and deeds all the rest of their lives. Most importantly kids need to "start small." By setting an achievable goal a child's enthusiasm will grow. By attempting a task destined to fail, the child will feel like a failure. So whether cleaning up one small area of the local beach, finding a home for one lost kitty, collecting juice boxes at one school lunch, or bringing one box of toys to a local shelter, kids will feel proud of their accomplishment and be ready to take it a step further next time.

A "Celebrate the Children" Party

The next time your school, neighborhood, church, or youth group wants to hold a fund-raiser why not have a Celebrate the Children of the World Party! Contact local cultural centers and museums for some ideas and recipes. Perhaps they might be willing to come and give a demonstration of a favorite activity, game, or food. Throughout the chapters in this book we have listed numerous multicultural activities and recipes that would be suitable—check the index for page numbers.

Our Community

Here are some ideas to get kids started in their corner of the world:

• Set up recycle bins in schools, churches, and at neighborhood parks. Twice a month organize a group of adults and kids to gather the cans and turn them in for cash to donate to a local charity of your choice. To set up a juice box recycling program contact Aseptic Packaging Council, 1000 Potomas St. NW, Suite 401, Washington, D.C. 20007.

• Donate excess fruits and vegetables from your garden to local homeless shelters, or better yet set up a community garden to supply fresh vegetables. Enlist the help of local garden clubs, Scout leaders, and teachers.

• Kids can donate books—perhaps those they've already read or that they have two copies of—in their name to the local library.

• Enlist the help of friends and neighbors to help round up and deliver unwanted books to the local library.

• Children make up a large portion of the population in women's and homeless shelters. Make up "Kids Care" packages to distribute. Some items to include might be stickers, markers, crayons, scissors, jacks, yo-yo's, and other small, inexpensive items to share with children who are less fortunate.

• Lend a hand with renovating or building a home for a needy family. Contact Habitat for Humanity, 121 Habitat St., Americus, GA 31709-3498. 914-924-6935.

• Write to Daily Bread in California for information on setting up a "Milk for Children Who Need It" program. Volunteers help feed the hungry through this nonprofit organization. Daily Bread, 2447 Prince St., Berkeley, CA 94705. 510-848-3522.

Our World

• Older kids and teenagers can spearhead a movement to be a "sister city," with the help and support of their mayor, city officials, and interested adults. Contact Sister Cities International, 120 S. Payne Street, Alexandria, VA 22314, for more information.

• Adopt a needy child from a foreign country. When sponsored by a classroom, Scout troop, or church youth-group, the adoption can cost each child just a dollar or two and can make a huge difference in the life of an unfortunate youngster. Contact Save the Children Foundation, 54 Wilton Road, Westport, CT 06880. 800-243-5075.

Autumn Afternoons

Though children spend most of their time in school during this season, kids and adults will enjoy these pursuits during after-school time, on the weekends, and during those unusually warm days of fall known as Indian Summer.

Bicycle Mania   (AGES 6 AND UP)

With winter fast approaching, kids will want to spend as much time as they can on their bikes! Create an Autumn obstacle course for added fun!

• Rake leaves into individual piles that are spaced 4 to 5 feet from each other. Draw a starting line with a piece of chalk and let kids take turns weaving in and out of the piles to the finish line. Time the contestants—the bicycler who rides the course in the shortest time (without falling into a pile of leaves!) is the winner.

• Play Bicycle Polo! Set up goals on either end of a big grassy area. Form teams and let kids kick a soccer ball with their feet while riding their bikes. We used to play this on the weekends, adults and kids!

Hoop and Pole Game (AGES 5 AND UP)

Here's a game that is perfect for Indian Summer and that was played by Apache men. Kids can play a similar version using a hula hoop as a target and a stick for shooting through the hoop. Two players run along parallel lines. One player rolls the hoop along in front of him, while the other player repeatedly throws the stick ahead of them on the ground, hoping to position the stick so that when the hoop stops rolling, it falls across the stick!

Homemade Flubber (AGES 5 AND UP)

Any child who's seen that wonderful Walt Disney movie starring Fred McMurray will want to try this magical goop! A kind of crazy Silly Putty, it bounces and lifts newsprint and will entertain kids for hours.

1 teaspoon 20 Mule Team Borax
5 teaspoons Elmer's Glue-All

Dilute the Borax in an 8-ounce glass of water. Stir to dissolve. Add the glue and mix until the mixture resembles silly putty.

A Simple Tin Lantern (AGES 6 AND UP, WITH HELP)

The sun loses its strength in the fall, and the days become shorter. Children can light up their autumn nights with this easy lantern.

Several lanterns of varying sizes look lovely grouped together and make an attractive centerpiece for family meals. (Candles should never be lit without close adult supervision.)

> *A clean tin can*
> *Hammer*
> *Various size nails*
> *Towel*
> *A piece of clay for securing the candle*
> *A short candle*

Remove the lid from the can. If the edge is rough, pinch it smooth with a pair of pliers. Fill the can with water and place it in the freezer until frozen solid. (This way the can will keep its shape when punched.) Remove the can from the freezer and place on top of a folded towel. With the hammer and the nails tap a design into the sides of the can. (Children may first want to work out a design on paper.) Leave about an inch of tin solid at the bottom to prevent the wax from leaking out of the holes. Empty out the ice and dry the inside of the can. Place the chunk of clay in the bottom of the can and secure the candle.

"Socks," the Hobbyhorse (AGES 5 AND UP)

Here's an easy hobbyhorse little buckaroos can put together in under an hour. It's great for riding through piles of leaves!

> *A heavy woolen sock*
> *Old socks, stockings, rags*
> *3-inch diameter wooden dowel, about 38 inches long*
> *Twine*
> *Glue*
> *Two buttons for "eyes"*
> *A black, waterproof marker*
> *Felt or yarn*

Tightly stuff the heavy sock with the scraps. Push one end of the dowel into the heel of the sock and continue adding stuffing as

Simple Fun

Make a simple "Pattern Matching" game from construction paper. Cut three different Autumn symbols out of colored paper: orange pumpkins, brown leaves, and white ghosts. Cut out about 6 of each symbol. Arrange from 3 to 6 assorted symbols on a work surface. Have the child match the "pattern." (Start with 2 or 3 symbols at a time for younger children; patterns for older kids may be more complex.)

needed, until the sock is full. Tie the bottom of the sock tightly with the twine, making sure none of the stuffing is visible. Glue the eyes in place and draw on other features. Glue felt or yarn in place for forelock and mane. A halter may be made from pieces of felt and glued in place if desired. Use additional twine for reins.

Index